TAKE TIME *for* GOD'S WORD

Phil –

Continue to be a great Blessing to others!

Stay Blessed!

David A. Pedersen

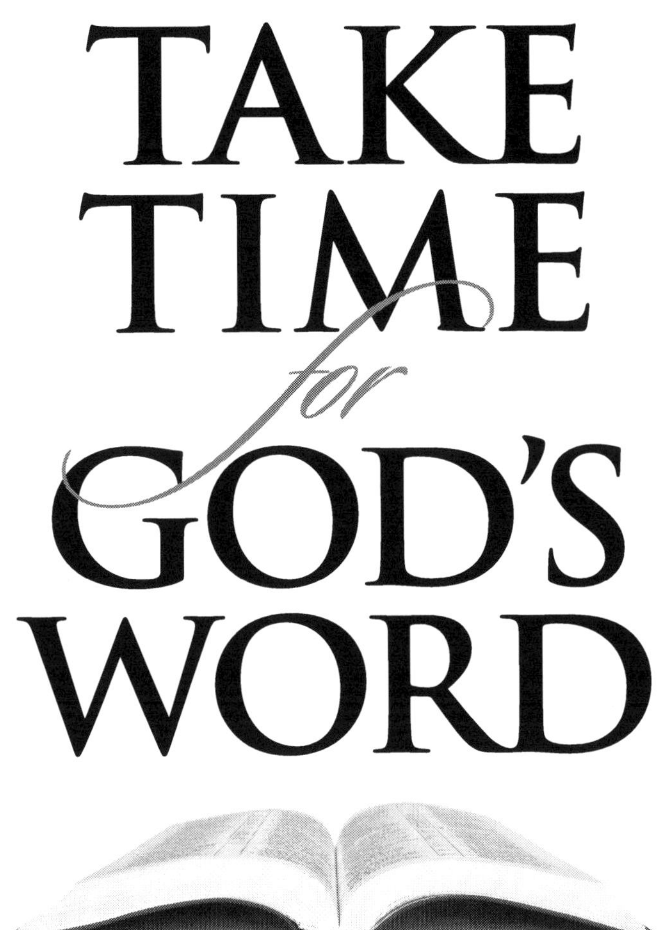

25 Easy Ways to Remember the Bible

DAVID A. PEDERSEN

Published by Prescott and Radcliffe Press. P.O. Box 191, Bloomingdale, IL. 60108. editor@taketimeforgodsword.com

Library of Congress Cataloging-In-Publication Data

Pedersen, David A.

Take Time For God's Word: 25 Easy Ways to Remember the Bible / David A. Pedersen

ISBN 13: 978-0-9981982-2-4 (print)

ISBN 13: 978-0-9981982-3-1 (ebook)

Dedicated to faithful parents and grandparents
who are sharing God's Word to the next generations of believers.
Stay blessed. Pass it on!!

Contents

PREFACE

Did you ever know exactly what you should be doing, but you did something else instead? Or, maybe you regularly lose sight of your top priorities? As a long time Christian, some people think my life must be easy. Well, while it has been blessed, it is NOT easy. So, after four decades of corporate executive roles in healthcare and software systems development covering three million air miles and the equivalent of seven years of hotel stays, I think I have learned quite a few lessons.. AND I hope that these teachings become a short-cut so that you do not take SO LONG to learn them yourself.

What I am about to share with you is about change. It is about goals. And, mostly it is about people like you and I who want to draw closer to God but who struggle to find the time.

The idea for this came to me many years ago, one night at **3:16 am**. I had a lot on my mind. Challenges at work. I had been fired from a long-time employer and had recently taken a new job. It was A LOT different than expected. I had to scramble to catch on to the tools, processes, and problems of the new firm. I was not as confident as I had been in the past. I needed to keep this job even if I wasn't sure it was the right fit for me at the time. So, it was not uncommon for me to wake up, in a sweat, in the middle of the night. But this time it was different. As I looked at the bright green numbers **3:16** on the digital clock near my bed, I immediately began to mentally recite John **3:16, "For God so loved the world that he gave his one and only Son, that whoever believes in him shall not perish but have eternal life."** (NIV) I then rolled over and, with that promise in mind, I fell peacefully back to sleep.

The next morning, I thought about what had happened in the middle of the night and recalled the time and the Bible verse. I realized that for some people, perhaps many people, relating the time of day to their 'chapter: verse' references may be the link or memory point they needed to stay close to God. I knew that is what I needed because I struggled with two problems. The first was truly taking the time to spend with God throughout my day. I knew some Bible verses but seemed to justify my focus on work and staying busy with my job by remembering the verse from Colossians 3:23 **"Whatever you do, work at it with all your heart, as working for the Lord, not for human masters,"** (NIV) and the verse from Ecclesiastes 9:10a **"Whatever your hand finds to do, do it with all your might,"** (NIV). My busy life was crowding out God. I could get to the end of a busy, frustrating, trying day and I could not remember praying or thanking God or anything other than the worries of work. I quickly realized that I could not do it all myself AND that I REALLY needed God's help throughout all the hours and minutes of my days.

The second problem was remembering God's promises from the Bible. Now, I may have known a verse BUT I could not remember where it was in the Bible. That was a problem for me. It meant I was less likely to share my faith because I was not comfortable or confident that I knew my Bible well enough. That day...all that changed for me.

What's more, <u>in less than 15 seconds, I can teach you how to follow this</u>

technique. It will make the difference in a verse being just 'memorable' to that verse becoming **'unforgettable'**!

Often we read a verse or hear a compelling verse being read but we don't focus on it or link it to something that will trigger that memory. On the other hand, everyone checks the time. Many of you check it constantly throughout the day. By linking time to key verses, we can then bring to mind those verses at those times throughout our day. Doing so keeps us close to God's Word. It reminds us that He is constantly with us. It reminds us to bring our prayers and thanksgiving to Him throughout the day and not just as a prayer of fatigue before crashing into bed at night. That became the beginning of **Take Time For God's Word©.**

I began my journey of Bible Study and cataloging key verses by their 'chapter: verse' (linked to Hour: minute) order as it may relate to time. There I found some key insights that may apply to you as well:

There are many more verses in the chapters 1-12 as there are many short books in the Bible. So, there are LOTS of great verses to remember that will become part of your everyday journey! The power of your linking and a little imagination on your part will anchor many verses to your memory throughout your day.

There are many more verses in the 1-30 range of verse numbers as there are fewer chapters with more than 30 verses. This means you will know MANY verses for some points in time. You can remember one OR all of them to help you through your day.

There are many great verses in books which have more than 24 chapters. As a result, this memory technique (like God himself) is not bounded by time. The reminder techniques can still apply but they need to be anchored in a different manner, as you will see throughout the book. I will show you how to relate verses to other things in your life AND it will change the way you look at some things KNOWING the verse that you have attached to it.

There is not a chapter: verse combination for every minute of every hour. I didn't expect there to be. And, this is not just a mechanical process of resequencing verses. This was and is my personal passion to find and to share and to help others become closer to God through His word. The phrase that I use to summarize it is: **"God's word...top of mind... close at hand...deep in your heart"** or another way to think of it is: **"Bring it to mind, take it to heart".** And my favorite is, **"You will carry these verses with you forever!"**

As Christians, we may face a variety of challenges and hardships in our lives. Therefore, I have organized verses into topics or themes which speak to God's Word about that topic. This may be about Pain, Testing of Faith, Blessings, Love, and other similar topics. You may find that you know many of the verses. That is fantastic! This process would help you to anchor them to a time or event and activity so that you bring them to mind more frequently throughout your day. They may be for comfort or strength or forgiveness or whatever may be your need at that time...literally at that time.

Now, if you are like me, if you can't think of a verse for that specific time, that's okay. Think of a verse for that hour ... Or just think of your favorite verse. The important part of this process is to **Take Time For God's Word.** That is the change! Making God a priority in your life throughout all the times in your life. Make knowing God more fully by knowing His Word more deeply to be your goal through this process. I am fully confident that our God will be there for you anytime, anywhere, day or night. My prayer is that you will remember to think about Him as He is always thinking about you!

I do pray that you will follow the processes and suggestions that are recommended in my book, on Facebook at www.facebook.com/taketimeforgodsword/ , or on my website at www.taketimeforgodsword.com. Use these references and 'helpful' materials to further reinforce your learning AND, because you will know more verses, you can use them as a witnessing tool to friends and family about the verses which you are learning and why those are important to you. As most of you know, sharing and teaching others what you are learning is the best way to make it truly a part of your life and your habits.

Enjoy the journey. Have fun in growing deeper in God's word. Share

His love and joy with others throughout your day. You may be the blessing that others are praying for today. Be that blessing!!

Just remember to **Take Time For God's Word**...often!

INTRODUCTION

Every new habit needs to create a pattern. It needs to be imprinted on your behaviors. It needs to be repeated often enough so that it seems natural and even easy to do.

That's how I've designed this Introduction. It will provide you with some GREAT verses with which you may already be familiar. It will help you visual them at their "time" on a clock. It will list the key words to get you started. Together, we will work through some trigger events or activities to help reinforce these verses. The next steps are up to you. You will need to try to <u>remember a verse for each hour that you check the time.</u>

I encourage Bible Study class students to initially use the printed paper (see Resources section for information/ instructions) so that you are looking at the verses frequently. You want this to be successful. That is why you invested in this book. You want to spend more time in God's Word AND you want that Word to become more a part of your life every day. You will find that sometimes, just a glance at the paper is all that is needed to trigger remembering the verse. Soon, it will happen automatically and you can file the paper away.

Getting Started

First, visualize an analog clock face. Then, visualize the hours/ minutes that go around the clock. (Not too hard so far!). Next, picture a specific verse for each hour around the clock. (See below).

As noted, there are only a few words associated with that verse reference number. These are the 'trigger words' which will help you get started with this verse. Often, it only takes a couple of words and the rest of the verse will come easily. There is also a Summary Chart of all the times/ verses so that you have it available to learn the verse or as a reminder of some verses which you are still learning. (See below).

Time	Book	Verse
1:09	**1 John**	***If we confess our sins,* he is faithful and just and will forgive us our sins and purify us from all unrighteousness. (NIV)**
2:08	**Ephesians**	***For it is by grace you have been* saved, through faith—and this is not from yourselves, it is the gift of God— (NIV)**

Time	Book	Verse
3:16	John	*For God so loved the world that he gave his one and only Son, that whoever believes in him shall not perish but have eternal life. (NIV)*
4:13	Philippians	*I can do all things through Christ who strengthens me. (NKJV)*
5:16	1 Thessalonians	*Rejoice always, (17) pray continually, (18) give thanks in all circumstances; for this is God's will for you in Christ Jesus. (NIV)*
6:21	Matthew	*For where your treasure is, there your heart will be also. (NIV)*
7:07	Matthew	*"Ask and it will be given to you; seek and you will find; knock and the door will be opened to you." (NIV)*
8:28	Romans	*And we know that in all things God works for the good of those who love him, who have been called according to his purpose. (NIV)*
9:24	Luke	*For whoever wants to save their life will lose it, but whoever loses their life for me will save it. (NIV)*
10:11	John	*"I am the good shepherd. The good shepherd lays down his life for the sheep." (NIV)*
11:28	Matthew	*"Come to me, all you who are weary and burdened, and I will give you rest." (NIV)*
12:12	Romans	*Be glad for all God is planning for you. Be patient in trouble, and prayerful always. (TLB)*

Reminder!

This book is organized around themes made up of groups of verses related to that theme. You may want to read it as a regular book, a chapter at a time and then find the verse(s) which you want to focus on most from that theme. The stories and illustrations about the verse and its context are intended to give you greater insights and to help make remembering the verse (and the time reference) even more memorable and easy. So, whether you read the book one verse at a time, one chapter at a time, or from beginning to end, the key is to read, associate, remember, and keep remembering those verses which help you in your daily living with Christ.

CHAPTER 1

Blessed to be a Blessing

When we think of being blessed, we think of happiness and having our needs (and a few wants) satisfied. That's okay. But God has plans to go much deeper and much broader than just our limited and local needs. Think MUCH BIGGER!

This brief theme is getting us tuned into the Beatitudes so that we don't just know them, but that we actually can live them. They are easy to remember as the trigger word(s) are ***"Blessed be*** (or ***are***)" which tells us who are blessed and what that means to them and to their calling in the world. So, what are you called to do or be? Do you feel blessed in that activity or position? Are you viewing it as a blessing to others? What can be done to make it that way in the future? These are just a few things to consider throughout this series. The more you think about them, the easier the words become and the more focused your efforts become to live out those words in your daily life.

Sometimes, it is best to start a topic with some definitions to make sure that we are on the same page in what we mean when we say a term like 'blessed' or 'blessing'. So, what does it mean to be '**blessed**'? Is it: 1) holy, sacred, 2) bringing joy, joyful, 3) happy, fortunate, and 4) enjoying the favor of heaven; beatified (i.e. 'the state of being made blessed'). Those are some of the definitions. Then, what is a '**blessing**'? Is it: 1) a prayer asking God to show His favor; a benediction, or 2) a giving of God's favor. We will look at these well-known verses with a new vantage point... that of being 'blessed to be a blessing'. As you read, review and remember them, find out which ones are really speaking to you... right now... right where you are in life... and, in God's plan, right where He needs you to be.

Our first two verses touch upon two of the greatest challenges we face in our world today, to be ***'poor in spirit'*** and ***'to mourn'***. So, 5:03 Matthew states,

5:03 ***"Blessed are the poor in spirit, for theirs is the kingdom of heaven."*** *(NIV)*

We have all heard stories and testimonies of people who have truly hit 'rock-bottom' in their lives (and maybe that describes you at one time)... desperate beyond their own abilities, talents, and means. They all come back to saying something like, "I had tried EVERYTHING... nothing worked... finally, I had nowhere else to turn, so I turned to God." While they had distanced themselves from God, He was still near to them. While it was a long-distance call for them to reach out to Him, He was just a whisper away from them. The ***'poor in spirit'*** are in a terrible kind of poverty. We have probably all had times in our lives when we were poor financially but were too happy to notice it. Here, for those without God, without the knowledge that they are children of God and heirs to a kingdom, their poverty of spirit leaves them in the worst place imaginable...that is without Hope! We are the people to provide them with the blessing of sharing the ***'kingdom of heaven'***... not only beyond death and the grave...BUT here and now. Are you giving that blessing to others?? My grandfather lived in Arizona and we visited them (from Iowa where I grew up) only every three years so I have fewer memories of him but very vivid memories of his faith and faithfulness. He would often quote one of his favorite hymns with the words, *"Count your many blessings, name them one by one. Soon it will surprise you what the Lord has done."*

Next in 5:04 Matthew, we see,

5:04 ***"Blessed are those who mourn, for they will be comforted."*** *(NIV)*

We most often think of this in connection with the death of a loved one... and that is a truly hard experience to go through. For Christians, while we can mourn their passing, we can also rejoice in knowing what's still in store for them and for us in the resurrection. But for those without that assurance...without that faith, they still need comfort and support... they need us to be there then, too. This is also mourning for other losses, not just death but lost dreams, lost fortunes, lost opportunities, lost love, lost jobs, and more. Our country has been in times of mourning in recent years. The world as we once knew it won't be that way anymore. In 2001, we saw that we were vulnerable to attacks right here at home. In 2008, we saw that bedrock financial and investment institutions which were thought to be 'too big to fail,' both failed and were failing to hold the confidence of the American and world investors. Are we being a blessing to those people in their real needs and in sharing our hope and our joy which can change mourning into rejoicing? Or, are we watching from the sidelines when those things happen and silently hoping that they 'get what's coming to them'... where are you in being a comforter to a nation and world who is still in mourning?? So, when you hear of a death or of a time of mourning, remember 5:04 Matthew, ***"Blessed are those who mourn, for they will be comforted."***

Then, 5:05 Matthew,

5:05 ***"Blessed are the meek, for they will inherit the earth."*** *(NIV)*

We don't use the word 'meek' much these days...there aren't many good examples, I guess... it means, 'to not be easily angered; gentle; mild'. So, do we view this 'inheritance' like an unexpected gift from a distant, long forgotten relative... OR is this the just rewards for a life of patience, forgiveness, and love? To 'inherit the earth' is to graciously accept ALL of the good and wonderful things that God has already given us here and now... to use them wisely as his good stewards... to share them generously with others in need...and to pass them on in good condition to the next generation and to those yet to come... until He comes again. As the words of one Christian song encourage us by saying, "Continue the work of the Lord; Continue to Praise His name; Continue to Thank the Lord; Until He comes again." So, let us be meek... not weak, in our attitudes as we carry out His will for us here and now!

3 Point Checkpoint

- ***5:03 "Blessed are the poor in spirit,* *for theirs is the kingdom of heaven."*** *(NIV)*
- ***5:04 "Blessed are those who mourn,* *for they will be comforted."*** *(NIV)*
- ***5:05 "Blessed are the meek,* *for they will inherit the earth."*** *(NIV)*

Our challenge is to not just read these verses but to anchor them into our memories and to recall them during the week. So, starting today at about 5 pm when the day's work is closing out...or at 5 am as you are starting an early morning, begin with these first 3 verses... ***'poor in spirit'...'mourn'...'meek'*** *and repeat them. They will become anchored into your thinking AND when you check the time, you will remember those as verses. How great is that!*

Then, each day, pay extra attention to see how you are 'blessed' and whether you were a 'blessing' to someone else. If we do this a few times, then we should have a different outlook on the days and weeks ahead. We should truly expect great things, and if we are watching for them, we will not be disappointed. For all too many of us, we experience some levels of disappointment each week.

Things didn't go our way...others were shown favoritism...or others pushed harder to get their own way. If we break down the word to 'dis' meaning 'not' or an 'opposite' of the word it is attached to (for example, 'believe' or 'disbelieve') and 'appointment' meaning 'a meeting with someone at a certain time or place'. So, to disappoint is 'to fail to keep a promise to another person'. I am sure we have all missed appointments that God has placed before us this past week... to say a kind word... to lend a listening and caring ear... to be the hands and feet of Christ to someone in need... to be the heart of Christ to offer a prayer for family or friends. That's the people Jesus was speaking to in the Sermon on the Mount (beginning in Matthew 5) and that is the same message of the Beatitudes to us today!

Blessed to Be a Blessing *(continues)*

Next is 5:06 Matthew,

5:06 ***"Blessed are those who hunger and thirst for righteousness, for they will be filled."*** *(NIV)*

Do you ever skip a meal? I don't mean snacking in between, I mean miss a real meal? How do you feel after a few hours? Kind of hungry, aren't you? Jesus was talking to a crowd of people who likely knew what it was like to miss meals, maybe a lot of them. There was no social or welfare system. If you didn't have work to do, you didn't get paid. Jesus wanted them to understand at a very personal and physical level the kind of deep desire he wanted for them to have in pursuing righteous living.

The word 'righteousness' means 'acting in accord with divine or moral law: free from guilt or sin.' *(Merriam-Webster online Dictionary).* We don't see our society emphasizing righteousness much anymore. Many consider it an outdated concept and yet we are seeing corporations and businesses needing to train their employees on ethics and corporate standards because people don't get any moral education if they aren't active in a church or religious program. Jesus wants us to recognize that when we get physically hungry or thirsty, then we are likely also in need of spiritual feeding as well. Getting to know God's Word personally and deeply will be a great resource for you to have in times of need and throughout your life. <u>It will be 'time' well spent!</u>

The Beatitudes continue at 5:07 Matthew,

5:07 ***"Blessed are the merciful, for they will be shown mercy."*** *(NIV)*

Jesus shared this message best in the parable of the man who owed the king a vast debt and when he pleaded with him to show mercy, the king did so and forgave the whole debt. The man left greatly relieved but then found a man who owed him a small debt and he would not relent until the man had paid back everything. The king was enraged by the man's actions and his lack of compassion on the other debtor. He had the man and his family imprisoned until their whole debt to the king was repaid.

While that parable is from the Gospels, it could be told today as well... about you and me. Our great debt and ALL of our sins have been paid by Christ on the Cross. Yet, we holdback that same mercy and forgiveness to so many others. Matthew 5:07 should be on our minds and on our lips at the end of every workday. Do we show mercy, forgiveness, and love to others? Did anyone notice a difference in our attitudes and our lives from those around them? So, say it often...live it always!

Moving on to 5:08 Matthew,

5:08 ***"Blessed are the pure in heart, for they will see God."*** *(NIV)*

The Bible talks about being pure and holy (i.e. set apart for God's purposes) as one of the highest forms of worship. Pure from a metallurgy perspective would mean that there are no contaminants or foreign materials within the sample. All of the molecules and atoms of that element, the tiniest parts of all, are exact and uniform and perfect...therefore, pure. But in this world, we most often get close, even very close to pure. Yet, there is always some minute particle which is not. It may be in the handling. It may come in the processing. It may even come from the storage. It gets SO close, but it is not quite there so it is not pure.

It was like the old (i.e. 1950s-1960s) Ivory™ soap commercials which claimed it was "99 and 44/100's" percent pure. Some of us may have glimpses of that 'being pure' moment but most of us realize that if it is only the pure in heart that will see God, then we need to cling to being redeemed by Christ as our reconciliation. For in knowing Christ, we will see God at work in our hearts. He is cleaning out the contaminants. He is refining the purity that is there and is putting it to the test. Graciously, He repeats that process again and again as we seek to grow closer to Him.

3 Point Checkpoint

- ***5:06 "Blessed are those who hunger and thirst for righteousness, for they will be filled."*** *(NIV)*
- ***5:07 "Blessed are the merciful, for they will be shown mercy."*** *(NIV)*
- ***5:08 "Blessed are the pure in heart, for they will see God."*** *(NIV)*

*Keep focusing on those keywords or trigger phrases to help you get started with a verse. When my young granddaughter is learning verses at church, she will often say, "I can remember it grandpa, IF you will help say it with me." Those keywords are the 'say it with me' part to help you get started with the verses. Think **'hunger'...'merciful'...'pure in heart'.** It will come to you with just a little focus and remembering to* **Take Time For God's Word.**

Blessed to Be a Blessing *(continues)*

Our next verse continues in 5:09 Matthew as it says,

5:09 ***"Blessed are the peacemakers, for they will be called children of God."*** *(NIV)*

In the late 1800s in the Wild West, it was the Colt .45 pistol which had the name of 'peacemaker'. I am pretty sure that the Biblical reference was not symbolic of that BUT in a real sense, a peacemaker often is the one who needs to get into harm's way to stop wars and fighting in order for peace to have a chance.

I remember listening to a voicemail message from our local high school that said our son had been involved in a fight at school. My heart dropped. I was quite surprised. It was out-of-character for our son to react or respond in that way. I was preparing a great lecture for him when I got home. When I called the school to get the details, it was 'clarified' that our son didn't start the fight and 'technically' wasn't in the fight BUT as he was trying to break-up the fight, the principal showed up...SO, it didn't matter the reason for being involved, each person had a part of the punishment. I did give him only 'part' of the lecture but it was more about doing what's right EVEN IF it may still get you in trouble. We need to arm ourselves with the ***'sword of the Spirit'*** which is the Word of God.

Continuing on to 5:10 Matthew, we find,

5:10 ***"Blessed are those who are persecuted because of righteousness, for theirs is the kingdom of heaven."*** *(NIV)*

In America, we talk about the church facing persecution from the media, the ACLU, from various government or judicial venues which are enforcing the letter-of-the-law in separating church and state...I often wonder, if we were to enforce the natural law and the statement that, ***"The earth is the Lord's, and everything in it, the world, and all who live in it."*** (NIV) (Psalm 24:1)... then where does that leave the 'state' for land or air or water...or people, for that matter. I think they should look beyond the statutes of Law when they are trying to decide where the boundaries of God and His laws or statutes should be set!

But, elsewhere in the world today, hundreds upon thousands of Christians are being directly and bodily persecuted for the Gospel's sake. People are imprisoned, beaten, and even killed because they profess the name of Jesus Christ to a people who don't or won't have anything to do with Christianity. We need to truly pray for those who face such dangers.

It is for us and greatly for those in other lands that this verse reminds us of our calling and prepares us for what will come, someday, in some way to all of us...and to remember ***'theirs is the kingdom of heaven'*** the same way that it was for those who were ***'poor in spirit'*** (Matthew 5:03).

Our final verse in this Blessed set of verses is 5:11 Matthew which continues with,

5:11 ***"Blessed are you when people insult you, persecute you and falsely say all kinds of evil against you because of me."*** *(NIV)*

In the media today, there are clearly lines drawn and cable/ TV/ radio stations set up to represent both very liberal and very conservative positions on politics, religion, and life or lifestyle choices. In a land where we do have 'freedom of speech' and 'freedom of the press', if you stand up for what you believe and what the Bible represents, you will be criticized and even ostracized by others who want nothing to do with any religion or lifestyle which implies any restrictions from the ME...MY...MINE viewpoints of today.

I have recognized that Christianity and naming the name of Jesus will not be popular in most circles but that to be true to what's true is more important than anything people may say or think about you. We just need to remember that verse 5:11 is like the events of that September day of 2001, 9/11 is not the final word...there is more to come from those dark moments...God would not let this end in defeat or desolation...there is the 'light of the world' yet to come.

3 Point Checkpoint

- ***5:09 "Blessed are the peacemakers, for they will be called children of God."*** *(NIV)*
- ***5:10 "Blessed are those who are persecuted because of righteousness, for theirs is the kingdom of heaven."*** *(NIV)*
- ***5:11 "Blessed are you when people insult you, persecute you and falsely say all kinds of evil against you because of me."*** *(NIV)*

Nine short verses. Some of the most quoted in the Bible. Some of the best to follow in living our lives. All have actions or consequences. That is what a Blessed life looks like. Living on purpose with a purpose. Knowing what to do and knowing the impacts of doing it. We often need to remind ourselves that in some situations, WE are the blessing that others were praying for. While the situation is tough or painful or frustrating or whatever emotion you may be feeling, you may have been put there for just the 'right reason' that God knew you could handle it AND that you would be blessing others through the person and character and love which God has built up in you. How great is that!! Blessings can happen in moments BUT the effect and the memories of them can last a lifetime. I would encourage you to be purposeful in creating those kind of memories for yourself, your family and your friends. So, Be Blessed to be a Blessing to others always!

When memorizing a series of verses, it is often finding and anchoring in the key words in each verse to establish that sequence. So, those words could be: ***Poor... mourn...meek... hunger.... merciful....pure... peacemakers... persecuted... insult****......and now we come to the last verse of all... it's not on your list and it is easy to remember... it begins with* ***Rejoice:***

5:12 ***"Rejoice and be glad, because great is your reward in heaven, for in the same way they persecuted the prophets who were before you."*** *(NIV)*

Four simple thoughts in the one phrase...

Rejoice and be glad,
for your reward is great in heaven,
for so men persecuted the prophets
who were before you

I was at a company training seminar on negotiating early in my career and by the end of it, the content was condensed down into about seven key words...

grouped into a formula... so after two days, they only hoped that we would remember the seven key letters of those words... PPVVCCI (Pain, Power, Vision, Value, Control, Cost, Impact) (as I recall). While interesting concepts and pretty memorable, I would much rather have the words and letters from Matthew 5 stick in my mind as those will last well beyond the years in my working career... those will last forever. So, take the list, highlight the words from each verse to remember the sequence... and remember this final verse. Look it up... read it a couple of times but make it part of the memory.

God tells us NOW what our reward will be and He tells us that the road will not always be an easy one... maybe not so well traveled with some bumps and detours along the way... BUT He has also told us that He is ***'the way, the truth, the life'****. Having Him in our lives should be all the blessings that we need to live that Blessed life AND to be a blessing to others. It is all there in a few verses if we will commit them to memory not just in our heads but in our hearts as we daily work to* **Take Time for God's Word.**

Through this series, we have focused on the Beatitudes with the theme **Blessed to be a Blessing**. *I know, for me, it is very helpful to just say the word 'Blessed..." and then a whole series of verses come to mind...mostly in order... but some are more pronounced than others in my memory. It has reminded me (again), just how truly Blessed we, as a nation, as a people, and as a church have been blessed.... So, now what? For some, they not only count their every blessing, they put them in boxes, bags, banks, or vaults to make sure they don't lose a single one of them. They get the 'blessed' part but they miss the 'to be a blessing' which is the greater emphasis and which is the most fun. Next we are going to focus on the word GIVE (and its variations). The theme is* **"Give – For Giving is Living."**

Blessed to be a Blessing–Summary

Time	Book	Verse
5:03	Matthew	***"Blessed are the poor in spirit, for theirs is the kingdom of heaven."*** *(NIV)*

Time	Book	Verse
5:04	Matthew	*"Blessed are those who mourn, for they will be comforted." (NIV)*
5:05	Matthew	*"Blessed are the meek, for they will inherit the earth." (NIV)*
5:06	Matthew	*"Blessed are those who hunger and thirst for righteousness, for they will be filled." (NIV)*
5:07	Matthew	*"Blessed are the merciful, for they will be shown mercy." (NIV)*
5:08	Matthew	*"Blessed are the pure in heart, for they will see God." (NIV)*
5:09	Matthew	*"Blessed are the peacemakers, for they will be called children of God." (NIV)*
5:10	Matthew	*"Blessed are those who are persecuted because of righteousness, for theirs is the kingdom of heaven." (NIV)*
5:11	Matthew	*"Blessed are you when people insult you, persecute you and falsely say all kinds of evil against you because of me." (NIV)*
5:12	Matthew	*"Rejoice and be glad, because great is your reward in heaven, for in the same way they persecuted the prophets who were before you." (NIV)*

CHAPTER 2

Give – for Giving is Living

When I did the Bible search (in the RSV), there were more than 1500 verses or references to the word 'give'. While I did not read each one of them, I did review many from the Old and New Testaments. Then, I realized that we could learn a lot about **Giving** right there in Matthew, starting only a few verses beyond where we left off in Matthew 5 from the prior chapter.

Let's start our journey into **Giving** in Matthew 5:16.

5:16 ***"Let your light so shine before men, that they may see your good works and give glory to your Father who is in heaven."*** *(RSV)*

During the weekly Bible Studies at our church, we have discussed some of the people who are making headlines today. Some are famous people. Some are people in the media whom others may look up to or may even idolize, to some degree. Some of these people have made terrible personal choices on habits, behaviors, and lifestyles which in prior generations would not have been tolerated. Now, it seems to be just another story... like so many others... that we don't even pay much attention to it. Contrast that with this verse from Matthew 5:16. Three (3) simple phrases in one sentence... (repeat the verse in the phrases shown below)...

"Let your light so shine before men,
that they may see your good works and
give glory to your Father who is in heaven."

As we read in the first sentence of *The Purpose Driven Life* by Rick Warren..."It's not about you." We quickly come to realize that our "light" is only a reflection of what Jesus has done and is doing in our lives. He is the Light of the World. Our "good works" are only the outcome of his outpouring of love, mercy, grace and forgiveness so that we can be free to be... to be a blessing to others. And if we do that, those simple but oh so difficult tasks, people will notice. They will be amazed. They will realize that our lives are not our own... that we belong to something and someone MUCH bigger than what is happening here and now. And, they will GIVE glory to God and thanks for His hand that placed us, near them, at this time and in this place. Your giving of yourselves will result in true living... and it will show.

Next is a verse from Matthew 5:42.

5:42 ***"Give to him who begs from you, and do not refuse him who would borrow from you."*** *(RSV)*

With all of the recent bailouts in banking, finance, car manufacturing and more, this could be tomorrow's headline, but I am sure the media would omit the reference to Matthew. In context, it is Jesus talking about just how far we are to go to respond to someone who is in need... verse 40 says... ***"if they take your coat, give him the cloak as well"***.... Verse 41 says, ***"if compelled to go 1 mile, go 2 miles."*** Then there is our verse 42: ***"Give***

to him who begs from you, and do not refuse him who would borrow from you." Verse 5:43 repeats what most people then and even today still believe and live by...as Jesus characterizes what our world teaches to "Love your neighbor and hate your enemy." All of which sets up the verse which turns our world upside down in verse 44, where he tells the people to ***"love your enemy,"*** ... ***"bless them that curse you"...."pray for those who despitefully use you and persecute you"***. In our culture, the media would say (and is saying)... that's just 'crazy talk.' But that's because the media really don't understand **giving**... they know taking... they know holding... they know hoarding...etc... <u>but not giving;</u> Jesus voluntarily gave his Life for us... so that we might live. So, use Matthew 5:42 to bring to mind the whole story... and then baffle the world by doing what God asks... ***"give to him who begs from you."*** <u>You may never see the returns in this life... but the rewards will be eternal.</u>

The third verse comes from Matthew 6:11. It is a verse which many of you have memorized and which you may say every week,

6:11 ***"Give us this day our daily bread;"*** *(RSV)*

It is right there in the middle of the Lord's Prayer. Such a short sentence that we breeze right past it... we are generally in a hurry to get to the "forgiveness" part of the prayer... that's what we know we need... forgiveness, and we do. But let's not overlook that simple request... our need for sustainment and nourishment, each and every day. Our need is there whether we seek His forgiveness or not. Without that generous gift of food, we would die. When I began searching for the word 'give.' there were many references in Genesis of ALL the things which God had given to mankind...God is a giving God....or we would not be here today. But in His giving, I believe that He is setting that model and standard by which we should judge our actions. Do we give as freely as He does? Or do we give only with an expectation on getting something?

For me, what started as giving an occasional gift of the $1 presidential coins (a commemorative series from the US Mint which began in 2007 to include the first 40 presidents) has now become a habit. At times, it is a social experiment as well. I find that there is a lot of suspicion about the gift, as some will ask, 'What's the catch… what's the gimmick… what do I need to do for it?' When I say there is none and I explain the nature of a souvenir…'a memento of a person, place or event. Something special, something to remember.' It is then that I get a small glimpse of the problem of the Gospel…the problem is that it is **free… a free gift from God through His Son, Jesus**. But you must accept it as a gift. You can't buy it, earn it, work for it, inherit it, etc. It is a personal gift which lasts a lifetime and beyond. Giving is in the character of God, but the world has trouble with that concept… that's why we need to demonstrate it to them in word and in action. Practice giving every day.

3 Point Checkpoint

- ***5:16*** *Matthew* ***"Let your light so shine before men, that they may see your good works and give glory to your Father who is in heaven."***
- ***5:42*** *Matthew* ***"Give to him who begs from you, and do not refuse him who would borrow from you."***
- ***6:11*** *Matthew* ***"Give us this day our daily bread;"***

At 6:11pm, just as you are beginning your evening dinner, pause an extra minute to remember how good God is in providing you with your daily bread… as we know it to be… and that is Jesus, the Bread of Life. Then as you can see from God… that 'giving is living'. I hope that you will use the sample set of cards (See Resources) to help remind you of that fact and that focus day-by-day, hour-by-hour and even minute-by-minute as you **Take Time for God's Word** *each day in your life.*

Giving (continues)

Verse 4 in the theme is from Matthew 7:02 which is a great verse for either the start of your morning (7:02 am) or as a reflection on how your day went (7:02 pm) and what could have been done differently or even better.

7:02 ***"For in the same way you judge others, you will be judged, and with the measure you use, it will be measured to you."*** *(NIV)*

This verse sounds a bit like the 'golden rule' which is from Matt 7:12 (NIV) ***"So in everything, do to others what you would have them do to you, for this sums up the Law and the Prophets."*** That comes just a few short verses later than where we are in 7:02. The first half of the verse is about judgement... what we pronounce or use, will be used in judging us. I have not been one to try to judge other people... too many variables... too many situations and circumstances which I cannot even begin to understand. And God challenges us not to judge other people... after all that is His job and He does it with perfect knowledge and fairness.

It is the second half of the verse which needs our attention the most. That says that ***"the measure you use, it will be measured to you."*** Our pastor and others have reminded us of a 'mother's way of defining sharing'... One child gets to divide the item in 2... the other child gets first choice. (It is amazing how evenly the item gets divided!)

My own illustration on this is patterned after a story and an example from Pastor Charles S. Mueller, Sr. which he told in Bible class maybe 15-20 years ago... but I still remembered it. Recently, I was returning to San Francisco to get on the Bay Bridge (old Bay Bridge before 2010). The 'Cash Only' line up ahead looked open so I drove for it. I mis-calculated that the road turned and that the long lines I was seeing were for that lane. There was no turning back. The best that I could hope for was to signal that I needed to get in that line and hope that there was someone who felt sorry for an 'out-of-town' driver who mis-judged the traffic lines and lanes. The first car to my right waved me to come into that lane... I was shocked! So as I approached the toll booth, I paid for 2 tolls... mine and the car behind me. (Like the story that pastor told about his daughter... good story... great idea). There was lots of traffic merging onto the bridge so I didn't see that car again. I don't know what they thought, or said to each other... but I know for me, and it has been true throughout my life, the measure you give will be the measure you get in return. Try it sometime (soon). I am more convinced each day that 'giving is living'.

Our next verse is found in Matt 7:11 (so that should be easy to remember each time you pass one... a 7/11 store that is).

> 7:11 ***"If you then, who are evil, know how to give good gifts to your children, how much more will your Father who is in heaven give good things to those who ask him!"*** *(NIV)*

The words leading up to this talk is about a child's request to his or her father. Ask for bread, he wouldn't give a stone. Ask for a fish, he wouldn't give a snake. So, if we can do the basic good things for our children, how much more will God be able (and He is infinitely able) to provide to those of us who are willing to ask... for we KNOW that He is a giving God.

There was a story in the book, *"Beyond Jabez"*, in which the author, Bruce Wilkinson, talked about people and places he has been since authoring the short book on the *"Prayer of Jabez"* (1 Chronicles 4:9 –10). In one story, it was about the planning for a huge outreach program to Africa... sending people to help plant local and family gardens as a way to reduce hunger and to help people provide more for themselves and their families. They had so many volunteers and people wanting to participate that they could not get enough seats on airlines to get everyone there to fulfill this mission project. Bruce had suggested that they need to pray for a 747 Jumbo Jet to be donated for use to that mission project... to many people, it seemed impossible... like that was just way too much to ask of God. It wasn't. They had a sponsor very quickly. People were amazed... but that is the kind of giving God we have... one who listens and responds... most often, even before we know to ask. So, what do you need to ask for today?

The sixth verse is from Matthew 10:08, (which is part of Jesus commissioning his disciples for their first mission trip, our focus is on the 'give' portion of this verse but the whole verse applies... maybe more than we know).

10:08 ***"Heal the sick, raise the dead, cleanse lepers, cast out demons. You received without paying; give without pay." (ESV)***

We can understand the part about...***"heal the sick"***. We have seen what that looks like in our lives. But the others... ***"raise the dead, cleanse the lepers, cast out demons"***... that seems to be way beyond our imaginations, let alone our comfort zones. And each of us is equipped in different ways with different skills. God created them and He will use them, to His glory and for His needs...IF we will just be available to His calling. And the focus sentence in the verse is, ***"You have received without paying; give without pay".*** (And he is not talking about pastors or full time church workers)... but about you and me. As I said in prior pages, a problem... maybe even THE problem with the Gospel message for many people is that it is FREE. Eternal Life is a free gift from God through Jesus Christ His Son. It's really a pretty simple message... BUT love, forgiveness, grace, and mercy from a giving God... that seems just too hard for many people to comprehend... it sounds too good to be true. But because it is God's plan, it is the only thing that we know and can trust to be true.

3 Point Checkpoint

- ***7:02*** *Matthew* ***"For in the same way you judge others, you will be judged, and with the measure you use, it will be measured to you." (NIV)***
- ***7:11*** *Matthew* ***"If you then, who are evil, know how to give good gifts to your children, how much more will your Father who is in heaven give good things to those who ask him!" (NIV)***
- ***10:08*** *Matthew* ***"Heal the sick, raise the dead, cleanse lepers, cast out demons. You received without paying; give without pay." (ESV)***

Three more verses with six 'giving' verses so far in this chapter. Which is your favorite? Which did you know already but forgot that you knew it (e.g. 6:11 from the Lord's Prayer)? There are 3 more still in this chapter... and hundreds more for you to look-up and read and remember as you continue to find your hope, your joy, and your direction in God's word, the Bible. **Take Time For God's Word** *this week in your life and every week from now until... forever.*

GIVING (CONTINUES)

The last 3 verses in the theme on **Giving** starts with Matthew 10:42.

> 10:42 ***"And if anyone gives even a cup of cold water to one of these little ones who is my disciple, truly I tell you, that person will certainly not lose their reward."*** *(NIV)*

When I think of giving, whether it is for Birthday's or Christmas, I usually start out with what 'big' thing do I think they want. I want it to be noticeable and in proportion to how much I care about that person. God's idea of giving is much bigger and broader... not in the size of the gifts, but in the size of the heart of the giver. In Jesus day, just like today, the Bible truth is still there... ***"The poor you will always have with you..."*** (Matthew 26:11a). He tells us that it is in the little things that people will see His hand of Love and Mercy the most... that ***"cup of cold water"*** to one of these little ones.

We get lots of Christmas catalogs sent to our home during that time of year... I don't know where they get our names, but they do. They all get thrown away except for one. I look forward to getting it each year even though I know most of the gifts in it by memory. It is a catalog from **World Vision**, a Christian outreach to some the poorest children in the world. And each year when my family asks want I want for Christmas, my answers are about the same... 'a goat, a dozen chickens, a couple of rabbits, some gardening tools and seeds, and maybe a couple of blankets'. (Gifts they can purchase to give to others instead of giving gifts to me directly.) I will likely never meet the people who get those gifts each Christmas, at least in this life, and that's OK with me. I would much rather have them see these as gifts from God which happened to be routed through me (or given by others from me) than to see my small part in it at all. The gift of Christ is all the Christmas present (and future) that I will ever need. Where are you planning to give that 'cup of cold water' today? Whose life will you help to change this week? What gift that you give will bring joy to others throughout the remainder of the year? Wherever and whenever you choose it, that gift will be welcomed by those in need and respected by God.

Next is a powerful verse from Matthew 13:12.

13:12 ***"Whoever has will be given more, and they will have an abundance. Whoever does not have, even what they have will be taken from them."*** *(NIV)*

In our society, we think in terms of the 'haves' and the 'have nots'. We like to stratify our incomes, homes, schools, lifestyles beyond the lower, middle, and upper to the 'in between' levels... like 'upper-middle' or 'lower-upper'. We think in terms of money, possessions, and 'stuff'. When God talks about abundance, it is about love, joy, peace, patience, humility, and all of the emotions which make a person truly feel like they have it ALL. We read about wealthy sports figures, movie stars, and business moguls who spend lavishly but can't seem to find any meaning or satisfaction in the things they acquire.

I often use this song's lyrics as a comparison to how we live and how God asks us to live. I heard it more than 40 years ago in college and it has stuck with me. It's called the **"Blond Christian Song"** and the words go like this:

"I haven't got a 40 foot yacht, I haven't got a lot of fame;
but what I've got is more than naught, for I name Him the 'name of Names'.

"Some people will tell you that if you are a Christian,
you really don't know all the fun that you are missin';
don't bite on their bait, let me set you straight, Christian's have more fun than Blonds (unless you are a Blond Christian)".

"Human nature has a tendency to take a little puff,
of pride and to say, 'I've got more than enough";
of the gray matter's wrinkle and green-backs crinkle,
but that just don't set right with God."

"Well, all I have or will be, was given me by Him,
who gave for me His life, and he hung it on a limb,
so cut out the strife, and enter new life,
so abundant it sloshes the brim." (Author is unknown to me)

Our last verse in this theme is Matthew 16:19.

16:19 ***"I will give you the keys of the kingdom of heaven; whatever you bind on earth will be bound in heaven, and whatever you loose on earth will be loosed in heaven."*** *(NIV)*

In this last verse, the emphasis is on what God is ready to give to you, now, this day, here on earth... ***"the keys of the kingdom of heaven"***. We've read about the 'pearly gates' and 'streets of gold' in references to heaven. So, the keys to that place seem pretty big and pretty important. But I am not sure they are the kind of keys that lock doors or gates... but rather the keys that open minds, and hearts, and lives to see Jesus Christ... even through you and even through me. What we bind on earth, what we give our life's effort and mission for, will be bound for heaven.

I have often mentioned in our Bible Study group about visiting my grandfather in Arizona when I was a young child. Sitting a bit cramped, with 8 people around a table for 4, as we would finish a meal and we would end with a song or favorite hymn of my grandparents. Some I didn't know at first but I learned them through the years and have not forgotten them since. The one that relates to this verse, at least to me is, *"Blest be the tie that binds our hearts in Christian love, the fellowship of kindred minds is like to that above." (by John Fawcett, 1740-1817)*

Yes, heaven is closer than you may think. We get to see small glimpses of it here and now. We actually get to bring it to others in various forms of our giving... A cup of cold water... Abundant giving freely and without restraint... And in the fellowship of believers... friends today and our 'forever' friends in God's plans for us.

3 Point Checkpoint

- ***10:42** Matthew **"And if anyone gives even a cup of cold water to one of these little ones who is my disciple, truly I tell you, that person will certainly not lose their reward." (NIV)***
- ***13:12** Matthew **"Whoever has will be given more, and they will have an abundance. Whoever does not have, even what they have will be taken from them." (NIV)***
- ***16:19** Matthew **"I will give you the keys of the kingdom of heaven; whatever you bind on earth will be bound in heaven, and whatever you loose on earth will be loosed in heaven." (NIV)***

*Please tuck these verses away in those memory banks or lock them deeply in your heart. Look at the reference card (See Resources) when you can't quite remember the verse but start by picking just one of the verses on 'giving' and make it your own... one that you repeat often and that you can use to remind you that we need to **Give – For Giving is Living**... in God's plans for your life each day as you **Take Time for God's Word.***

Giving–Summary

Time	Book	Verse
5:16	Matthew	***"Let your light so shine before men, that they may see your good works and give glory to your Father who is in heaven."*** *(RSV)*
5:42	Matthew	***"Give to him who begs from you, and do not refuse him who would borrow from you."*** *(RSV)*
6:11	Matthew	***"Give us this day our daily bread;"*** *(RSV)*

Time	Book	Verse
7:02	**Matthew**	***"For in the same way you judge others, you will be judged, and with the measure you use, it will be measured to you."*** *(NIV)*
7:11	**Matthew**	***"If you then, who are evil, know how to give good gifts to your children, how much more will your Father who is in heaven give good things to those who ask him!"*** *(NIV)*
10:08	**Matthew**	***"Heal the sick, raise the dead, cleanse lepers, cast out demons. You received without paying; give without pay."*** *(ESV)*
10:42	**Matthew**	***"And if anyone gives even a cup of cold water to one of these little ones who is my disciple, truly I tell you, that person will certainly not lose their reward."*** *(NIV)*
13:12	**Matthew**	***"Whoever has will be given more, and they will have an abundance. Whoever does not have, even what they have will be taken from them."*** *(NIV)*
16:19	**Matthew**	***"I will give you the keys of the kingdom of heaven; whatever you bind on earth will be bound in heaven, and whatever you loose on earth will be loosed in heaven."*** *(NIV)*

CHAPTER 3

Give Thanks

This theme is about giving **THANKS** and the message title could be expanded to say, **Give Thanks...for He is our hope and our joy!** As you likely noticed, the last 2 themes and verses were all from Matthew. Matthew 5 was the series on **Blessed to be a Blessing.** Our last set of verses, also all from Matthew, was on **Give... For Giving is Living.** We will be using verses from across the Old and New Testaments on this theme of emphasizing the words **Give Thanks.** It is fun to look through a wide range of verses to find the ones which I hope will be most memorable to you and which will become part of your **Take Time for God's Word©** storehouse of verses for sharing and as a reminder of all that God, through Christ has done for us.

We start in the first chapter of 1 Corinthians with verse 1:04,

1:04 ***"I give thanks to God always for you because of the grace of God which was given you in Christ Jesus,"*** *(RSV)*

How many people in the world are today, this very day, giving thanks to God for **<u>you</u>**.... 1, 10, a hundred, or is it millions? Do you believe that there are millions of Christians around the world praying for us, as American Christians, praying for our safety, our support, and our ability to withstand the temptations and turmoil which we see daily in our land? Or, we could turn the question around and ask, 'How many people are you praying for?'... just your family? Maybe a few friends in need? Maybe our leaders and soldiers overseas? But are you praying for the 'whole Christian Church on Earth'? Saints in other lands who are living and dying for the sake of the Gospel.

I most often catch myself still confining the powers of God into just my little space and my limited view of His world. Thanks we give should be a BIG word covering so many things that we should be mindful of. In Norwegian, if you had a special meal or someone did a great favor for you, the expression was "tusen takk" which means 'a thousand thanks'... but, in our family, as the grandparents passed the language on to the children (our parents), we also added the word 'mange' (the word for 'many') to it so it was 'mange tusen takk' or 'many thousand thanks'. I think that is where we need to be in our lives.... Speaking the words to Christ... those words of giving thanks as 'mange tusen takk' giving thanks for thousands (upon thousands) of his people. We are not alone in our faith.

In Paul's verse, it was likely that his thanks are for a few handfuls of followers that he left behind in Corinth, after all, it was only his first trip there. But those numbers grew and grew. They continued to grow because of 'the grace of God"... and we should all know that 'grace' can be remembered by the acronym '**<u>G</u>**od's **<u>R</u>**iches **<u>A</u>**t **<u>C</u>**hrist's **<u>E</u>**xpense'... or, with just the understanding that it is **'undeserved favor'** which comes to us from God... His good grace to us. And we get that grace, not by anything that we are, or do, or have, or know, or can buy... It is **ONLY** given to us in Christ Jesus. So, we start our lesson and learning to **Give Thanks** by remembering to give thanks to God for those around us, those who have been given that grace to know who Jesus is in their lives... <u>That knowing makes all the difference in the world.</u>

Our second verse is from the book of Jonah 2 verse 9,

2:09 ***"But I with the voice of thanksgiving will sacrifice to thee; what I have vowed I will pay. Deliverance belongs to the LORD!"*** *(RSV)*

We all know the story of Jonah. We have read it and heard it many times. Our church pastor even took us through an audio and visual journey to get an even better understanding of the story, the setting and the re-telling of that great 'whale-of-a-story' as some from outside the church like to call it. I would greatly encourage you to memorize this verse, as it just may save your life. To our collective human knowledge, I am only aware of one person, Jonah, who was swallowed by such a 'large fish', lasted 3 days inside, and came out alive and well. And the reason this verse is SO important is, that it was the last thing that he said to God before the 'fish' threw him up onto the shores.

I know many people go through life looking for that fictitious *'Get out of Jail Free'* card... like in the game of Monopoly™. In this case, it was the act of giving thanks, in advance, that showed to God that Jonah had truly repented and was ready to do what God had commanded.

And it is not just the 'thanksgiving, it was also Jonah's commitment statement, **"what I have vowed I will pay".** Many churches and denominations have 'commitment' drives which ask their members to commit their time, talents, and possessions to God in the coming year. Are we as confident as Jonah to give thanks in advance, when we are still inside the fish, in some dark moments, to make bold commitments with thanksgiving? And then with that final line, **"Deliverance belongs to the Lord."** We have for decades heard the line in the Allstate Insurance™ commercials... "you're in good hands with Allstate"... but do you truly know and feel each and every day that you are in the cleft of His hand...(where 'cleft' means 'hollow part').. an opening just <u>your</u> size? So, we likely won't have many 'memory verses' in the Book of Jonah, but this is still one to keep. Keep giving thanksgiving in advance. Keeping our commitments to God (e.g. ***"what I have vowed I will pay"***). <u>And knowing that our true and only</u>

<u>deliverance from sin and death must come from God, through Christ.</u>

Verse three for this theme is from the book of Daniel 2:33 which tells us,

2:33 ***"To thee, O God of my fathers, I give thanks and praise, for thou hast given me wisdom and strength,..." (RSV)***

As we grow older, we continue to see that others, our age and younger, are preceding us in death. Some have even commented that they have more friends in heaven than they may still have on earth. I know for me, whenever an aunt or uncle passes away, I always think that I need to pray even more now than before, because I knew that they were praying and giving thanks for our family members. As those 'prayer-warriors' go home to the Lord, who will take their place? So, it is a reminder that the God of our fathers has been good to us and through that goodness and His countless blessings that I need to give Him the thanks and praise He deserves.

In Daniel's case, here was a young man taken into a foreign land. Unlike most, he was given a rare opportunity to be trained and educated with other young men in that country. He was shown favor by the king and as a result, he was given unique opportunities to give witness about his faith to a conquering king and to a pagan nation. He did so in quiet, consistent, and humble ways BUT those actions spoke powerfully to the leaders and eventually to the king. The message was clear and unrepentant, that Daniel's thanks and praise and faith was in one God, the God of Israel, Jehovah, the Most High God. He gives thanks to God for the wisdom and strength that he needs to survive in a 'foreign land'.

Some days when I go into stores, it seems that I am in a 'foreign land'... as the signs are in Spanish, or Polish, or Hindi, or Chinese... all with English subtitles (I live in the Chicago area). As Christians, we need to be looking for the 'subtitles' in our world to read and understand the message(s) from God that seem to be hidden to the masses OR are just lost in all the clutter, confusion, commercialization, media overload, and constant bombardment of messages of 'me, mine, and now'. We don't seem to be a society that is expecting the return of a Savior any time soon… only the 'returns on investments, 401k's, and bank account increases'.

I recall having had to laugh at all of the attention given to the movie and book(s) about the Mayan calendar of events and the 'end of the world' predictions for the year 2012; more specifically 12/21/2012. And while I laugh because the Bible is so clear that ***'no man knows the end time, only the father'****….* The good news was that people were really asking the question, if the 'end does come', then what will I do… where is my hope and my salvation. That was a good 'wake-up call' for many. Others were still oblivious to the facts that this world will end one day, and then there is eternity. Why this was so funny for me, in the worldly sense, it would have been 'poetic' after 40+ years of hard work and long hours that the first day that I become eligible for retirement (12/21/2012), also would become the end of the world. In the world's view, that would just seem so unfair. But in the Christian view, I am getting to enjoy small slices of heaven on earth, every day. Whenever that end comes, it will not be with a sense of regret or fear, but only the final sense of seeing Jesus face-to-face… forever.

3 Point Checkpoint

- ***1:04** 1 Corinthians* ***"I give thanks to God always for you because of the grace of God which was given you in Christ Jesus,"*** *(RSV)*
- ***2:09** Jonah* ***"But I with the voice of thanksgiving will sacrifice to thee; what I have vowed I will pay. Deliverance belongs to the LORD!" (RSV)***
- ***2:33** Daniel* ***"To thee, O God of my fathers, I give thanks and praise, for thou hast given me wisdom and strength,…"*** *(RSV)*

As you start your early afternoon each day, make sure that you are remembering to Give Thanks by remembering these verses or the ones that follow. Thanks-giving is more than just a day on the calendar. It is a way of living which provides more blessings than you can hold…so they spill over to those around you. What a great way to live out your life each day. Stay blessed!!

GIVE THANKS *(CONTINUES)*

We find the 4th verse in the theme of **Thanks** in John 6:11, *(Also, remember the 6:11 from Matthew...also about bread.)*

> 6:11 ***"Jesus then took the loaves, and when he had given thanks, he distributed them to those who were seated; so also the fish, as much as they wanted." (RSV)***

In the *Living Bible*, it says, ***"They ate until they were full"***. This is a great meal-time verse (**6:11**). Maybe this week at mealtime, you can practice it with your family or friends and by end of week, you will all have it memorized. More importantly, you will have focused on the importance of giving thanks, even as it was for Jesus, as a sign to us of how much we owe our thanks to God in all things great and small.

Now, you do need to remember that this is the story of the feeding of the 5000. And, you should remember the humble beginnings of this meal. Most of us think of Thanksgiving when we have a big meal and are REALLY full. We spend days polishing off the leftover turkey, dressing, yams, and deserts from a big meal (with LOTS of leftovers)... but it started as a BIG meal. In John chapter 6, it started with a small boy's lunch consisting of five barley loaves and two fish. That likely would not even qualify as an appetizer at your dinner party. But, for Jesus, it was more than enough. He gave thanks for the small things, knowing that God can make great things from even the smallest of faith... not the faith of Jesus, but the small and growing faith of his disciples. He gave thanks and then he distributed it to those disciples to see the miracle happen through their giving as well.

Growing up in our house, my dad learned that he needed to pass the food to the left (towards the youngest kids first), otherwise, my oldest brother would take 'his fair share' and there would not be enough for everyone else. In Jesus economy, it really didn't matter. Everyone ate (and ate) until they were full... until they had ***'as much as they wanted'***. That's still how Jesus gives today... full measure, bread and fish, all that we need.

But for many, they want little or nothing from Jesus...and that is what they are getting. They are starving for that 'bread of life' but they believe they can be sustained on what the world is feeding them. Soon, they feel empty again. They only need to ask and that 'full portion' is theirs... ***'as much as they wanted'***...if only they wanted more. So, how about you? Are you taking ***'as much as they wanted'*** from what Jesus offers you this day? Are you getting a taste but not really sitting long enough to get the full portion he has planned for you? Do you walk away from Church or your fellowship group 'full' or did you only want a couple of bites... just enough for the week... that's all.

This story ends with 5000 men (plus women and children) being fed until they were full AND there were TWELVE (12) baskets left over. There was still an abundance available even after all were fed. Now that's how we should be in our giving thanks.... Thanks for the abundance yet to come.

Our next verse is in Romans 6:17,

> 6:17 ***"But thanks be to God, that you who were once slaves of sin have become obedient from the heart to the standard of teaching to which you were committed," (RSV)***

As Christians, (and for some of us as Lutheran Christians), we like to spend more time talking about mercy and grace than we do about sinning. Oh, we recognize that we are sinners, but we really don't like to get into the details. That gets kind of personal and we know that God has already forgiven it through Christ's blood, so why even bring it up at all. Paul needed to be very clear to the young Church starting in Rome that God, through Christ, had worked a miracle to bring them from their former state, as ***"slaves of sin"*** to a new position.... to that of becoming ***"obedient from the heart"***. He wanted them to recognize how far from God's love and grace they once were, and what a change had taken place in their hearts. A change that could only come from knowing who Jesus is and what Jesus had done for them.

He goes on to talk about the ***"standard of teaching to which you were committed".*** Paul wanted to again impress upon them that while they were beginning to learn about Christ, it was just a beginning. There was a need for them to continue to seek him more each day and to spend regular time in His word and in fellowship with others. It is that same reminder to us today. To be ***"obedient from the heart to the standard of teaching to which we are committed".*** Now that is something to truly be thankful for... Are you? Do you express it each day??? Something to consider as you are reminded of this verse each day at dinner time. Romans **6:17**.

Next, we see that the verse numbers are increasing even as we now look at Psalms 7:17,

7:17 ***"I will give to the LORD the thanks due to his righteousness, and I will sing praise to the name of the LORD, the Most High."*** *(RSV)*

When I did my search on the word 'thanks', this verse or variations of it came up in Deuteronomy, Isaiah, and other Old Testament books. This was a common theme and an expression of thanks that was part of the Jewish traditions. It was an honest recognition that we need to give God thanks just for His righteousness. As we know from Paul's later writings, and his self-admission, ***'There is no one righteous, not even one;'*** *(Romans 3:10 NIV)*... Paul knew, as we know, that there is nothing and no one we can think of on earth who is even close to being compared with God and His righteousness. To be 'righteous' means, "the quality of being right and just". We often talk about a person who is 'self-righteous', meaning that what they do seems right in their own eyes. But, we know that God's version of righteousness is truly 'right and just' for that is the nature and quality of God.

This verse in Psalms continues, ***"and I will sing praise to the name of the Lord, the Most High"***. Again, this phrase is a common one (and therefore, it should be easy to remember). We probably don't appreciate the phrase 'sing praise' as much in our time and place... as we have radio, CDs, iPods, MP3 players, etc. so we have music with us and around us all the time. In David's day, it was a skilled musician who played an instrument or who sang to bring music or praise to God. It was an act of worship and it took planning, practice, and preparation.

Growing up in a small town in Iowa and working in my dad's gas station after school, I got to meet many of the townspeople as customers. I remember one older gentleman, Ben Hake, but everyone called him 'hummer Hake'... he was hard of hearing but he ALWAYS had a smile on his face and if you stood close to him, you could hear him humming one of many favorite hymns... always humming... perhaps, he thought it was just to himself, but everyone around him knew differently. I think the two expressions went hand-in-hand... a smile on his face... and humming his favorite hymns. To me, that is the expression of ***'sing praise to the name of the Lord, the Most High'.*** And the Psalmist always added, ***'the Most High'***.... Just in case anyone ever forgot, which Lord or which God we were talking about, there can only be ONE that is ***'the Most High'***. So, while we like to think of God, 'here with us', and He is through the Holy Spirit, we also need to recognize that there is only ONE God, the Most High. And with that position, He surely deserves our thanks and praise, continuously through how we live our lives.

3 Point Checkpoint

- ***6:11*** *John* ***"Jesus then took the loaves, and when he had given thanks, he distributed them to those who were seated; so also the fish, as much as they wanted."*** *(RSV)*
- ***6:17*** *Romans* ***"But thanks be to God, that you who were once slaves of sin have become obedient from the heart to the standard of teaching to which you were committed,"*** *(RSV)*
- *7:17 Psalms* ***"I will give to the LORD the thanks due to his righteousness, and I will sing praise to the name of the LORD, the Most High."*** *(RSV)*

Three more verses about Thanks... with the focus not on the person giving thanks but on God who is worthy of our Thanks and who gives us so much to be thankful for. As we have a (USA) holiday of Thanksgiving, let us make sure that it is not the only day we stop to give thanks. Giving thanks to God should be a regular part of our daily prayers and our lives should reflect that 'attitude-of-gratitude'... and may many of us earn the nickname of 'Hummer' as we keep a song in our heart so much so that we just can't keep it all inside of us, as we **Take Time for God's Word** *in our lives... it just must overflow to others.*

GIVE THANKS *(CONTINUES)*

We find our 7th verse in this theme in Mark 14:23,

> 14:23 ***"And he took a cup, and when he had given thanks he gave it to them, and they all drank of it." (RSV)***

This is another familiar verse. We hear it, or variations of it, every time we have communion. It is consistent with the verse from the prior section from John **6:11** about the feeding of the 5000. Jesus again shows his signs of submission to God in pausing to give thanks. It was also an example of how his disciples then, and his disciples today, need to live.

Do you remember to pause and give thanks at every meal... or are you half-way through eating when someone asks, "Did we pray already?" and no one can seem to remember. Or, when you are in a public place or out with non-Christian friends, do you still remember to bow your head and give a word of quiet 'thanks' to God for all that he has done... or, do you justify not doing it because 'it just wasn't convenient'. Is that the message you are sending to those friends or to your family? That 'giving thanks' is only for times when it is safe, private, or convenient? We are commanded to ***"give thanks in ALL circumstances"*** (1 Thessalonians 5:18). We learned that from Jonah (while he was still inside the whale) and from Daniel (while still in exile in a hostile land). We learned verses where they still gave thanks because it was right to do so. And it still is today.

We need to recognize that this nation, while founded by people escaping **from** religious persecution, has become a nation of religious (at least Christian religion) intolerance, if not persecution. We need to show our faith, knowing that it will not be popular at times... but it is OUR faith and we are called to express it, with thanksgiving. Now while I asked you to make **6:11** (John) part of your mealtime 'Take Time' list... this verse should also be on that list, too.

Verse eight is from 2 Chronicles 16:34,

16:34 ***"O give thanks to the LORD, for he is good; for his steadfast love endures forever!" (RSV)***

This was another familiar verse which I found throughout the first 5 books of the Old Testament. You have likely read it or heard it often in the past. Now we want to anchor it into your daily living (as **16:34** (24 hour clock time) is 4:34 pm). It was an earnest reminder to the people to 'give thanks' and a further reminder that God's promises do not fail and ***'his steadfast love endures forever'.***

When buying products today, the careful shopper always asks about the 'warranty' on the products they buy (and even from the shops or manufacturers who produce them... will they still be in business if there is a problem). We want to know that we are protected. Careful shoppers are also checking out 'web sites' to see what the 'reviews' are from other buyers which rate products on value, durability, customer service, etc. Still others are checking the 'recall list' or the 'safe-toy' list to determine everything they can know about a product...costing $50, $100, or $200. Yet, it is sometimes those same people who say they don't have time for 'religion' or 'God'... as if they don't care about any guarantees after this life. It seems very strange to me how some people can so easily focus on protecting the temporary (like toys) and miss the eternal as they rationalize away God in their lives.

That is why the people of Israel then, and Christians today, need to keep reminding ourselves, our children and our friends, that God is good... AND his steadfast love endures forever... well beyond the warranties on the caskets we will be buried in or the resting place of our ashes. That is something to truly be thankful for! AND then, He has promised that the best is yet to come... and we ask, "how good will it be??" He says it is hard to describe because there are really not good comparisons here on earth. So, while I continue to describe those 'glimpses of heaven on earth' as the hugs of a grandchild, the giving to others, and the peace which comes from knowing Jesus, those are only the 'best' examples we have as comparisons.... <u>We do know that we will be in the presence of God, so, what more could we ever ask for?</u>

Finally, the last verse in this theme is from Luke 17:16,

17:16 ***"and he fell on his face at Jesus' feet, giving him thanks. Now he was a Samaritan." (RSV)***

I know what some of you are thinking, what kind of a memory verse is that... it seems like there is something missing in it. So, two things: first, most of what we have learned are full verses and they could become memory verses but it's really about the message in the verse that's key, and, second, as our pastor has said about our mission as a congregation, and "Devoted Bible Study" that it's not about the 'memorization'... it's about LIFE. This verse is about life and a lesson we need to know.

Now, the verses before this are about the story of the 10 lepers. This was not a parable. This was a miracle from Jesus and the results of that miracle. You likely know the story. Ten lepers called out to Jesus for a healing; he had compassion on them; he told them to go and 'show themselves to the priests' (which was a requirement AFTER you had been healed of leprosy); and they did... and the priests said they were healed; they rejoiced and went on their ways... to friends, family, homes, businesses, etc.; except for one man. His story is captured in our part of this short verse, just 17 words that 'say it all' about this man and his character and his 'attitude-of-gratitude'. It says ***'he fell on his face at Jesus' feet, giving him thanks.'*** He was so grateful at the great gift (the gift of life...with the cleansing of his leprosy) that he fell at his feet... giving him thanks. And then comes the punch line, ***'Now he was a Samaritan'.***

Jesus healing reached beyond just the Jewish people. He healed all who truly asked. Then Jesus asked him, in following verses... weren't there 10 that I healed... where are the other nine?... this man didn't know... he only knew that he must give thanks to Jesus for the miracle he provided. Jesus then sent him on his way. So, my question for you is, "how many miracles have you asked for?"... then God granted them to you... then you managed to forget to acknowledge it and to return thanks to him.

As I have said before, my catch phrase and philosophy is: **'I just don't believe in miracles, I COUNT ON THEM!'** And I try to give thanks both in advance and after they happen... and they do seem to just keep coming.... Because ***'his steadfast love endures forever'.***

3 Point Checkpoint

- ***14:23*** *Mark* ***"And he took a cup, and when he had given thanks he gave it to them, and they all drank of it."*** *(RSV)*
- ***16:34*** *2 Chronicles* ***"O give thanks to the LORD, for he is good; for his steadfast love endures for ever!"*** *(RSV)*
- ***17:16*** *Luke* ***"and he fell on his face at Jesus' feet, giving him thanks. Now he was a Samaritan."*** *(RSV)*

Three last verses about Thanks. Nine short verses in all. Verses from all over the Bible to show that giving thanks is what we need in our lives every day. If we stop for even a minute, we will see yet another reason to give God thanks. As we leave this theme of ***Thanks****, it is hard to separate it from the next theme which is,* ***Praise****. This theme was created near the Christmas season but applies throughout the year (as you can still sing Christmas carols in July or anytime). We often think about Praise at Christmas when the angels above, and the lowly shepherds, and the learned wise men all stopped to recognize the significance of Jesus birth and to give God the Praise for that great gift. As you are hurrying about your day, regardless of the season, please be like the Samaritan who stopped and returned to Jesus feet to give thanks and when you have that minute,* ***"Take Time for God's Word"*** *as a way to* *get closer to him through these verses and the advice, support, and lessons that we can gain from them.*

GIVING THANKS–SUMMARY

Time	Book	Verse
1:04	1 Corinthians	***I give thanks to God always for you** because of the grace of God which was given you in Christ Jesus, (RSV)*
2:09	Jonah	***But I with the voice of thanksgiving** will sacrifice to thee; what I have vowed I will pay. Deliverance belongs to the LORD!" (RSV)*
2:23	Daniel	***To thee, O God of my fathers, I give thanks** and praise, for thou hast given me wisdom and strength, (RSV)*
6:11	John	***Jesus then took the loaves,** and when he had given thanks, he distributed them to those who were seated; so also the fish, as much as they wanted. (RSV)*
6:17	Romans	***But thanks be to God**, that you who were once slaves of sin have become obedient from the heart to the standard of teaching to which you were committed, (RSV)*
7:17	Psalms	***I will give to the LORD the thanks** due to his righteousness, and I will sing praise to the name of the LORD, the Most High. (RSV)*
14:23	Mark	***And he took a cup, and when he had given thanks** he gave it to them, and they all drank of it. (RSV)*

Time	Book	Verse
16:34	**2 Chronicles**	***O give thanks to the LORD, for he is good;*** ***for his steadfast love endures forever! (RSV)***
17:16	**Luke**	***and he fell on his face at Jesus' feet,*** ***giving him thanks. Now he was a Samaritan. (RSV)***

CHAPTER 4

Give Praise

As you can see so far, this is a progression of verses. We have been **BLESSED** and we are to then be a BLESSING to others. We must learn to **GIVE** because GIVING is real living. We need to remember to give **THANKS** to God for all His love, mercy and grace. And now, we need to **PRAISE** him for that great love shown to us in Jesus. Keep up the great job of remembering prior verses while learning new ones. While I am sure you have many favorites already, who knows but that your new favorite just might be in the themes yet to come. <u>Keep going. You can do this!</u>

Our first verse for the theme is from Joel 2:26. (We don't find too many real memory verses from Joel.)

2:26 ***"You shall eat in plenty and be satisfied, and praise the name of the LORD your God, who has dealt wondrously with you."*** *(ESV)*

In our country and our towns, we don't really appreciate the words ***'eat in plenty and be satisfied'*** because most people have more than enough on our plates at special meals (like Thanksgiving and Christmas) and at most every daily meal. And we have pantries, cabinets, drawers, or refrigerators/ freezers filled with even more food. In Jesus day, and TODAY, throughout the world, those six words, ***'eat in plenty and be satisfied'*** sound a lot like heaven-on-earth for the children searching garbage dumps for scraps of food. Or for those who eat grubs, beetles, or snakes because that is the only food they can find. We forget that millions upon millions will end this day desperately hungry for their next day's food, if it can be found. So, with all the abundance which we have, do you still take time to ***"praise the name of the Lord your God"*** and it is not just for the food, but as the verse continues ***"who has dealt wondrously with you".***

Now, I have never been a real card player, maybe some games of *Rook*™ , or *Authors*™ (if you can even remember that game), or a quick game of *Fish*™ with the grandkids. But today, on multiple cable channels, there are championship poker games going on, all the time. And they are announced with great drama and suspense as people wait for that next card to be drawn to fill out the hand and to see who will likely win, based on percentages... but the cards don't care about percentages, they come up when they do and sometimes people need to 'take the hand that is dealt to them'. So, if your life were like a game of cards, what kind of a hand have you been dealt?? You know that's the way the world sometimes views it... people get dealt good or bad 'hands'... and that's what they live with.

Fortunately, our God did not make us in that way or place us in this time and in this place as a 'random' deal or the 'luck of the draw'. We are placed here both 'on purpose' and 'for a purpose'. And one of those purposes is so that we can give him Praise, as the Doxology says: 'praise God from whom all blessing flow, praise Him all creatures here below, praise Him above ye heavenly host, praise Father, Son, and Holy Ghost'. So, today, remember Joel 2:26...to ***'eat plenty*** (*but healthy, I'm sure it was intended to be in there someplace)* ***and be satisfied'***... ***'praise the name of the Lord our God'***... and remember that he has ***'dealt wondrously with***

you'. Then say an extra prayer for those who are still in need... for He also hears our prayers... and He is gracious to act.

The next verse is from Luke 2:13 which I am sure many people will remember hearing frequently during the Christmas season.

2:13 ***"And suddenly there was with the angel a multitude of the heavenly host praising God and saying," (ESV)***

Wait, that is where the verse stops but it is not the whole story, so let's finish it together, with verse 14: ***"Glory to God in the highest, and on earth peace among men with whom he is pleased!"*** Many of us know the Christmas Story from Luke chapter 2 pretty much by heart... maybe not by memory, but we have heard it told and retold for 10, 30, 50, or more years. We know the sequence and the roles that each of the characters had in that first Christmas story. Some of us have played many of those roles in Christmas pageants as kids OR as 'grown up kids' (more or less) here at Trinity (or in your home churches) when we have the 'do-it-yourself' Christmas pageants. I always remember the angel's role with the Shepherds. That glorious announcement about the birth of Jesus, to some poor, uneducated, and frankly quite smelly shepherds. It's like his Map Quest™ or Google Maps™ was off a few miles and he missed the turn he should have taken.

My college roommate and I taught a high school Bible Study at the Lutheran Church we attended in Ames, Iowa, and we did a skit about that first Christmas and the angel's announcement. Only in our version, the shepherds did not get up and go, they settled back down to a good night's sleep...and we asked, "What would have happened to Christmas?"... What if that announcement came to you??? Would you get up... middle of the night and walk miles away looking for a newborn with no more description than ***'you will find the baby wrapped in swaddling clothes and lying in a manger'....*** I am not sure that even Google Maps™ could find it with those directions. But the shepherds went, and saw, and praised God for that miracle which they witnessed and returned to their flocks... and they continued to tell that great story to their children, their grandchildren and to anyone who would listen.

So, how about you? You have seen that same great miracle. Are you still telling others about it and passing it on to the next generations for them to tell to their children? That's why the angel was joined with the ***'multitude of the heavenly hosts praising God'***... they too could not hold back their high praise to God for doing this wondrous and miraculous thing for mere humans... the lowly shepherds and even the smartest wise men. It spoke to all peoples and resounded in heaven, as well. When I listen to the Christmas choirs, I can almost hear that angel chorus for it is with that same heart, and soul and voice that Christians around the world are retelling Jesus birth again each year... and let us all pray that it will be retold again and again, until He comes again!

The 3rd verse is continuing the theme of **Give Praise** from Luke 2:20,

2:20 ***"And the shepherds returned, glorifying and praising God for all they had heard and seen, as it had been told them."*** *(ESV)*

Many of us can relate to that first part of the verse, ***'and the shepherds returned'***. Same thing today, after Christmas, it's all about those 'returns'... the stuff that wasn't the right color, or size, or brand, or it's a duplicate... or 'what-were-they-thinking' with that gift? While the present was given with the right attitude, it just wasn't a fit or it didn't meet expectations. For those shepherds, they returned ***'glorifying and praising God for all they had heard and seen'*** for what they saw in the manger was that 'perfect gift' from God. It was that 'long expected savior' who had been promised to his people almost since the beginning of man's time on this earth. Yet, he came at ***'just at the right time'***, when the ***'fullness of time had come'*** all part of God's perfect plan and perfect timing... just the right gift for us, an imperfect people.

These lowly shepherd's, the ones who protected the sheep with their very lives...the one that Jesus identified himself with when he said, ***"I am the Good Shepherd, the good shepherd lays down his life for his sheep"***

(John 10:11 (NIV)). I am sure it would have been comforting for the shepherds to know that Jesus, the Lamb of God, that sacrificial lamb, was also called the Good Shepherd. Their attendance at that First Christmas was only the beginning for God to call out to those who were far away from the kingdom of God to be brought into that sheep pen for safety, for feeding, and for care. Who do you know today that is perhaps far away from the kingdom of God at Christmas or at any time during the year?? Family, friends, distant relatives, co-workers? Let's take seriously the offer from our local churches to invite others at Christmas time to 'Come Home for Christmas'... back to the manger where it all began... with hope, joy, promise, and most importantly fulfillment... that payment for our sins so that we may have eternal life with Him. It is the only 'present' with a future in it. Think about it. And invite others to share in that joy. But don't wait until Christmas, invite them this week.

3 Point Checkpoint

- ***2:26** Joel **"You shall eat in plenty and be satisfied, and praise the name of the LORD your God, who has dealt wondrously with you." (ESV)***
- ***2:13** Luke **"And suddenly there was with the angel a multitude of the heavenly host praising God and saying," (ESV)***
- ***2:20** Luke **"And the shepherds returned, glorifying and praising God for all they had heard and seen, as it had been told them." (ESV)***

Three verses about Praise. Some new, others very familiar... but maybe not thought of often enough... so maybe it needs to be more than just once each year. There were many, many verses on Praise throughout the Old and New Testaments so it is an important theme to go think about often. In the Resources are links to the website where there are bookmarks, folding verse cards, refrigerator signs to stick them under refrigerator magnets as a reminder, or just leave them on the kitchen table to re-read and remember with meals. You won't forget those meals... and you should not miss the opportunities throughout your day to ***"Take Time for God's Word".*** *Think of it as taking God's gift to you, through his word, and then making it your present to yourself, to store up those words... as it says usually at the top or bottom of each set of verse cards, "God's Word... top of mind... close at hand... deep in your heart... when you need it most."*

GIVE PRAISE *(CONTINUES)*

The next verse is from Acts 3:08 which tells us,

> 3:08 ***"And leaping up he stood and walked and entered the temple with them, walking and leaping and praising God." (ESV)***

First did you catch that this was from the book of Acts... so this healing was not from Jesus as those are reported in the Gospels... and yet it was from Jesus through the apostles who were carrying out the Great Commission from Matthew 28:19-20. Those verses are used within ***Take Time For God's Word*** with the 'stop light' visual (because there aren't 28 hours in a day... although some days that would really come in handy). The stop light visual was linked to the word **"GO".** And the verses say, ***"Therefore go and make disciples of all nations, baptizing them in the name of the Father and of the Son and of the Holy Spirit, (20) and teaching them to obey everything I have commanded you. And surely I am with you always, to the very end of the age." (NIV)*** Those disciples who were afraid on Good Friday were now standing up in front of the rulers of nations and were proclaiming the Good News of Jesus Christ. They were healing the sick and those who had been crippled for years, as was the case with this man.

The earlier verses talked about this man... crippled from birth at the gate of the temple... asking for money. Peter asked the man to look at him. Peter said, we have no money but that he would give him something else. Then he commanded the man, in the name of Jesus Christ of Nazareth, ***walk.*** Peter reached out to help the man up... as he had NEVER ever walked in his life... and then comes our verse. So, my question to you is, 'How many of our prayers are for money... and how often does Jesus remind us that he has something else, something even better for us to receive.' While many of us may be past the age of leaping, at least not more than a few inches, but our spirits and our hearts should leap for joy and praise when we just pause to look back on ALL the miracles that Jesus has given us through the years and that we know 'the best yet to come'. Now that is praise worthy!

The next verse is a real favorite of mine, and maybe yours as well from Philippians 4:08.

4:08 ***"Finally, brothers, whatever is true, whatever is honorable, whatever is just, whatever is pure, whatever is lovely, whatever is commendable, if there is any excellence, if there is anything worthy of praise, think about these things." (ESV)***

So, what do you think about on those days leading up to the end of a year... shopping, wrapping presents, getting the Christmas cards sent before Christmas this year... or maybe it's about the Christmas meal and worrying if it will turnout well... or maybe about the family coming home and going through the list of topics which are off limits to discuss, that is if you want the meal to be a peaceful one.

I like the verse because of the progression of words. Words are powerful and the sequence of them makes a big difference in how you choose them and in how you use them in your own mind. It starts with '***whatever is***':

- **True...** no false teachings, lies, or excuses... just the True thoughts from deep in your heart.
- **Honorable...** because it is true, doesn't always mean that we should dwell on it... it now takes a step up the ladder of our thinking to be 'honorable'.
- **Just...**we often refer to judges as 'the honorable so-and-so' and then it goes a step higher to their review of the facts and circumstances to move up to what is 'just' as in our word 'justice'.

- **Pure...**again, raising the bar a bit higher as to the motives behind our thoughts to weigh them and to see if they have been 'refined as if by fire' to be truly pure.
- **Lovely...** still moving up that ladder to assure that these thoughts which were even pure are also grounded in and bound in Love.
- **Commendable...** beyond lovely, we know what 'grace' means to us...grace is 'not getting what we do deserve' but Christ made us to be commendable to God ... so do you think grace and live grace in your daily thoughts?
- **Excellence...**near the top of the ladder of thoughts... it is excellence... that highest and best thinking... well beyond good or great... and finally at the top is...
- **Worthy of Praise...** top of the charts... highest level of thinking... do you work your way up the ladder to get to those thoughts that are Worthy of Praise...the way that God has shown Christ to be... worthy of praise.

Then the last part of the verse says, ***"think about these things"...*** so, if these are not on your list of thoughts today, maybe we need to start a new list and work our way up the ladder of things to think about... then that 'other list' will just fade in comparison. There are still things to do, but not necessarily things to take up our precious 'thought time'. That time when we can be praising God for ALL that he has given to us in His Son, Jesus. <u>Now that is something to think about... more often.</u>

The next verse in this set is from the last portion of Nehemiah 5:13 which says,

5:13 ***"...And all the assembly said "Amen" and praised the LORD. And the people did as they had promised." (ESV)***

The word **'Amen'** means <u>'so be it'</u> or <u>'may it become true'.</u> The verses leading up to this event were about Israelites taking advantage of other Israelites. They were taking their land and enslaving their children to pay off their debts, while the rich officials in the government just got richer. They didn't seem to care about their brothers and sisters. It was all about them. Or, did I read that same kind of story in today's Chicago Tribune... it sounds so familiar. These officials were called to task by the prophet. They recognized how far they had drifted away from the promises from Moses and Joshua about the Promised Land for ALL of the people of Israel... not for some to lord it over the others. The prophet told them of the curse that would come to them if they failed to do what God was commanding them to do.

And then in verse 13, we have the ***'amen'*** and they ***'praised the Lord'.*** Their recognition of doing wrong and of plotting evil against each other was turned around. It is kind of like our last verse about the ladder of words that lead up to the '***worthy of Praise***' theme. This group of leaders got the message. They changed. They ***'praised the Lord'*** and ***'the people did as they had promised'***. I am sure we would all like to believe that is what our elected officials are doing on our behalf... *that they did what they had promised.*

But in our world today, we don't have all of the people worshipping and respecting what God has planned for them. As a result, we have too many people who want to do it 'their way'... and we continue to see the consequences. We can only ask that we, as Christians, will not just think on those prior words from Philippians and Nehemiah, but that we will act on them and share them in our town councils, in our school boards, and in political circles of both parties. We are still the last, best hope for this country to not give up on our prayers, our praise, and our thanks for the blessings which we have every day. Then we need to continue to defend and protect those blessings from above, even if there are people who want to silence the message... just as Herod tried to do after Jesus' birth and as they tried to do again at the crucifixion. He could not stop the plans of God and people today cannot stop those same plans... unless we allow them to do so. So, let us also say ***Amen... praise the Lord...*** and ***do what we have promised...*** to spread the Good News of Christ's salvation to the world in need. To that, we can say, **Amen!**

3 Point Checkpoint

- ***3:08** Acts* ***"And leaping up he stood and walked and entered the temple with them, walking and leaping and praising God." (ESV)***
- ***4:08** Philippians* ***"Finally, brothers, whatever is true, whatever is honorable, whatever is just, whatever is pure, whatever is lovely, whatever is commendable, if there is any excellence, if there is anything worthy of praise, think about these things." (ESV)***
- ***5:13** Nehemiah* ***"...And all the assembly said "Amen" and praised the LORD. And the people did as they had promised." (ESV)***

Three more verses... some are easy to remember... just very hard to live out in our daily lives. It is not that we need to know them all, just that we work to live out those that we do know. We need to have that same 'song in our hearts' throughout the year as we do for the Christmas carols that just seem to pop into your head and you just start singing them because of the joy and the message that they bring. Even in these busy days, we need to ***"Take Time for God's Word"*** *and then take time to share it in thought, in word, and in deed. There are so many ways to reach out each Christmas season, don't think that the best presents come wrapped in a box or in a bag; the best present came in a small manger and still comes to us each day through His word.*

One quick story. My sister hosted the family gathering and planned a brief 'kid's program' with the grandchildren ages 17 months to 6 years. There was a little angel (the 17 month old... Emily) and a Mary, Joseph, shepherds, 3 Wiseman, even the pet dog played along as the 'animals'... type casting I'm sure. About 2/3 of the way through the reading from Luke 2, little Emily (the angel) decided she could wait no more, so she reached in and grabbed the baby (as a doll) and started hugging that doll and 'giving love' (kisses) to that baby. So, after the family re-gained composure at the impromptu disruption and baby Jesus was back in the manger, the pageant finished. But, afterwards, I wondered just how many of the 'multitude of the heavenly host' must have had that same feeling... seeing Jesus, the Son of God, so little and fragile and cold lying in the manger...

how many of them who would have gladly picked Him up and given him love the way that little Emily did to that doll. So, beyond the great and funny memory, the lesson to all of us is... don't leave the baby Jesus in the manger. Pick him up into your life and give him the love and the praise and the thanks that he so richly deserves and see him as your redeemer who has bought you with a great price and claims you as his own. He is the present with a future!

Give Praise *(continues)*

Our seventh verse for our theme is from Romans 14:11,

> 14:11 ***"For it is written, "As I live, says the Lord, every knee shall bow to me, and every tongue shall give praise to God". (NET)***

We often think of Christmas being tied to this **Praise** theme and perhaps it is still fresh in our minds, with all the Christmas carols, decorations, long lines at the return counters, asking ourselves, 'where are we going to put all of this stuff'. It seems like the 'peace on earth' has quickly become the question of 'can you believe this weather... how cold... how much snow... and how warm it would be in Florida or Arizona.' And for some of us (up north), we know how warm it is there... because friends who are down there keep calling or emailing us to tell us how warm it is.

The cares of our everyday lives seem to have caught up to us already... just as they did in Paul's time as he spoke to the Romans. Only here was a people who had no concept of God, at least the loving kind who would send his Son to die for us. But, Paul was able to get their attention when he started with ***'For it is written. 'As I live, says the Lord'***... which gave the people notice that God is not a 'dead god of times past'... but rather a 'living God for this time and for times yet to come'.

Paul further emphasizes that the sovereignty of God applies to ALL people and says ***'every knee shall bow.... Every tongue shall give praise to God'***... that is a theme we will see repeated in Revelations verses very shortly. And the most sobering verse comes next in verse 12, which states, "***So each of us shall give account of himself to God.***" So, what will your account be? Maybe a good husband or wife... good father or mother... at least we tried to be. OR, will it be that solemn acknowledgement that Jesus gave us that great gift, that only he could give, and because of that great love, we have inherited eternal life. We know that in the end, God will be given praise... let's keep practicing it now, while we have time.

The next verse draws us back into Exodus chapter 15. It is good to see how there were times when the people of Israel 'got it' and expressed their hope and their joy in God. From Exodus 15:02 we read,

15:02 ***"The LORD is my strength and my song, and he has become my salvation; this is my God, and I will praise him, my father's God, and I will exalt him." (ESV)***

The first half of the verse should take about <1 minute to read and then to remember. Many of us have heard it often, just like the children of Israel had. But it is surprising how quickly they forgot it... maybe, like many of us, who will get busy with the week ahead. I like it because it talks about ***'my salvation'***... it gets personal... it states a commitment. In the second half, it states, ***'this is my God and I will praise him'***... no one can do it for you... it is yours to decide... while a gift from God, you still need to open the present and to make it your own. It ends with ***'my father's God and I will exalt him'.*** Their fathers were Abraham, Isaac, and Jacob of hundreds of years before. They had now mingled and mixed with the Egyptians for hundreds of years so they had the 'memory of God' passed down to them but it was the miracles of God and the leadership through Moses which caused them to make a commitment... one which they would break several times along the journey.

It has been as our pastor describes for them and for us; a time of the people's promises; their failings and forgetfulness; their eventual recognition of those sins and shortcomings; God's mercy and restoration; and then the cycle begins again. So, while you can associate this with time (e.g.

3:02 pm), I also associate it with exercising. As pushups get harder each year, I am gratefully reminded that *'the Lord is my strength and my song'*, and he IS my salvation.

Finally, the last verse in this theme on **Praise** comes from the last book of the Bible, Revelation 19:05 which reminds us,

19:05 ***"And from the throne came a voice crying, "Praise our God, all you his servants, you who fear him, small and great"." (ESV)***

With any New Year comes new calendars and for some people, fresh resolution(s), perhaps too quickly broken. I am reminded of a good technique for changing the way we live by breaking our time and our priorities down to the question, "if I had one month left to live, how would I spend my days?" Rather than the traditional year-long promises or the promise to 'change for a lifetime'... but just not starting today... this question poses a short-term, practical, thoughtful and mindful way to structure our days and our interactions with family, friends (and enemies), work, church, etc. For those who have tried it, they say it has changed the way they live and they live each 30 days in the same way... on purpose... because it gives them a focus on their purpose in life.

As Revelation (and Romans) have reminded us, we all will praise God at that final day... no questions about it... no options... no choices or recall votes. It also reminds us ***'all you his servants'***... we are His Servants and when we see that for ourselves, it takes a heavy load from us as we are not the Masters, but the servants. The verse further states that to all of us... ***'you who fear him'*** and this is for some, the definition of 'afraid, terrified, shaken'... for others of us, it will be some of those reactions but with that added meaning of 'a reverent respect', knowing that he is our Father, in heaven.

And the final words, bring it all together for me.... ***'small and great'.*** I have often referred to the 'great' in the world's eyes... the sports figures, actors, singers, politicians, world leaders, etc. who on that last day will have no more excuses or armies or boundaries or ideologies or philosophies or theories upon which to rely... they will be there with the smallest, the humblest, those with that child-like faith that I mentioned in the 'kid's Christmas pageant' earlier. We will all praise him for who He is... God of the heavens and the earth and we will know him through his son, Jesus.

3 Point Checkpoint

- ***14:11*** *Romans* ***"For it is written, "As I live, says the Lord, every knee shall bow to me, and every tongue shall give praise to God". (NET)***
- ***15:02*** *Exodus* ***"The LORD is my strength and my song, and he has become my salvation; this is my God, and I will praise him, my father's God, and I will exalt him." (ESV)***
- ***19:05*** *Revelation* ***"And from the throne came a voice crying," Praise our God, all you his servants, you who fear him, small and great." (ESV)***

There you have it... from the New Testament letter to the Romans to the Old Testament great celebrations in Exodus to the foreshadowing of the end times, we will Praise our God. Keep those verses close at hand and in your heart so that we continually are reminded of how great is our God and how worthy He is of our praise.

Give Praise – Summary

Time	Book	Verse
2:26	Joel	***"You shall eat in plenty and be satisfied, and praise the name of the LORD your God, who has dealt wondrously with you." (ESV)***
2:13	Luke	***"And suddenly there was with the angel a multitude of the heavenly host praising God and saying," (ESV)***

Time	Book	Verse
2:20	Luke	*"And the shepherds returned, glorifying and praising God for all they had heard and seen, as it had been told them." (ESV)*
3:08	Acts	*"And leaping up he stood and walked and entered the temple with them, walking and leaping and praising God." (ESV)*
4:08	Philippians	*"Finally, brothers, whatever is true, whatever is honorable, whatever is just, whatever is pure, whatever is lovely, whatever is commendable, if there is any excellence, if there is anything worthy of praise, think about these things." (ESV)*
5:13	Nehemiah	*"...And all the assembly said "Amen" and praised the LORD. And the people did as they had promised." (ESV)*
14:11	Romans	*"For it is written, "As I live, says the Lord, every knee shall bow to me, and every tongue shall give praise to God". (NET)*
15:02	Exodus	*"The LORD is my strength and my song, and he has become my salvation; this is my God, and I will praise him, my father's God, and I will exalt him." (ESV)*
19:05	Revelation	*"And from the throne came a voice crying," Praise our God, all you his servants, you who fear him, small and great." (ESV)*

CHAPTER 5

Be a New Creation

He makes all things new! That seems to be a fitting start at the beginning of a New Year or even the beginning of a new day. So, if you were looking for that great time to change, don't wait for a new year (or a new decade and definitely don't wait for that next new century), <u>now is the time</u>. The good news for all of us is that he makes us new each day... and that is something to really look forward to.

We start this theme in the book of Ecclesiastes 1:09.

1:09 ***"What has been is what will be, and what has been done is what will be done; and there is nothing new under the sun." (ESV)***

And, I am sure most of you can see why we don't really have many memory verses from Ecclesiastes. It doesn't sound like a great new way to start a New Year or a new beginning. But, in reality, for billions (yes, with a "B") of people on earth, that is the way they are starting this year and this day... that is without hope, the kind we get from knowing Jesus. And we need to step back and remember who wrote the book of Ecclesiastes... who? It was Solomon, the wisest man who ever lived. He wrote many verses which talked about the vanity or uselessness in just pursing wisdom for that did not bring a longer or more joyful life. This came from a man who "truly had it all".

And what did he say as a recap at the end of that book, from the *New Living Translation* it says, in chapter 12, verses 13-14, ***"That's the whole story. Here now is my final conclusion: Fear God and obey his commands, for this is everyone's duty. God will judge us for everything we do, including every secret thing, whether good or bad."*** (NLT) Even with those final words, if it was at all based on our own merits and accomplishments, it would still not be 'good news' for any of those billions of people, including us. So, that is why we will look into other verses of the Old and New Testaments which talk about that 'truly Good News' and how he makes all things, including us, new. <u>Now that is a great beginning.</u>

Next, let's go back to Luke 2:10, and the reason I say back is because we saw verses in Luke 2 a couple of times in the **Praise** theme that focused more on verses from the Advent and Christmas seasons. It just goes to show that those verses are NOT just for Christmas, but for the whole year long... just like those favorite Christmas carols, it's OK to sing them even in July (and I often do). Luke 2:10, as you may likely already know it, states,

2:10 ***"But the angel said to them, "Do not be afraid. I bring you good news that will cause great joy for all the people." (NIV)***

We often talk about the first things out of an angel's mouth (at least when speaking to us humans) is ***"Fear not"*** or ***"Be not afraid"***. An angel, a being that serves daily in the presence of God, causes us to fear. Unfortunately, in our world, Christians are getting that same kind of reputation (and it is not for being angels)... but for causing other people to fear, not us personally, but what we represent. We are sharing the Good News... a message of love, joy, peace, and eternal life. With all of that, you would wonder why on earth that would cause people to fear... but it is not the Gospel they fear, but the fact that they would need to change... to repent... to repay... to seek others forgiveness... to confess their sins... to come clean. It is just easier to hide in the darkness than it is to come into the light.

So, when people seem to reject you because of your faith or your words about Jesus, it is just what they did to Jesus when he was here on earth. They feared him so much, that the wisest of them, the Jewish leaders, had him killed, not because he would change the whole world BUT because he would change THEIR world. The people who have heard the Good News from those angels do have great joy (while for some of us it doesn't always show through every day)... and it is a joy worth sharing.

I sometimes accuse my daughter of being a great Apple™ iPod/ iTouch/ iPhone™ salesperson, as she is telling others what it can do, she does it with great excitement... 'amazing sounds, colors, applications, so cool, etc.' I don't know how many went out and bought them just because of that excitement... and 'that it's easy enough for a three-year old to use it' (really... it is). While for many of us, the "Good News" at times seems like the Old News as we have heard it for 10, 30, 50 years or more... but it is not about us. For the rest of the world out there, this is not just Good News, it is the Best News they will ever hear. Let us not be so content that we know it that we forget or neglect to share it with others... tell them 'a little angel told you so'.... From Luke **2:10**, he did!

The 3rd verse(s) in this theme are from Lamentations 3:22 and 23.

3:22 ***"The steadfast love of the Lord never ceases, his mercies never come to an end; 23 they are new every morning; great is thy faithfulness."*** **(ESV)**

You may have heard variations of the first verse (v22) from your own minister or Bible readings so it should be easy to remember even though it may be phrased a bit differently. It is the next short phrases which reflect the theme of 'new' that we want to focus on. Those are:

"The steadfast love of the Lord never ceases,
his mercies never come to an end;
23 they are new every morning;
great is thy faithfulness.

The first phrase ***'his mercies never come to an end'*** is best illustrated in a quick story of two judges, both were caught for speeding so they decided to try each other's cases. The first got up, pleaded 'not guilty' and the judge said, 'Ticket rejected. Next case'. They switched places, the new judge asked how did he plead, he said, 'not guilty' and the judge said "$50, next case". The second judge was shocked, and he asked why? And the seated judge said, 'there has been a lot of that lately and we need to set an example'. Fortunately for us, God's mercies don't end and don't change based on how many sins have been piled up before Him from us or from others before us.

Next it says, ***'they are new every morning'***. We often jokingly hear that there are two kinds of people... those who wake up and say, "Good morning, God' and the others who say, "Good God, morning?" For Christians, it is always a good morning with God, regardless of what time of day that is.

And the verse ends with the way the last theme ended...***'great is thy faithfulness'***. With the 'great recession' (i.e. 2008), as some are now calling it, a recent and deep memory for many, people did not look forward to 2009, at least economically. We had great hopes for a new leader in the White House but we knew that the problems were bigger than just one person... this was a world-wide problem. As Christians, we are always thinking about the 'world-wide problem' of people trying to cope, to struggle, to even find hope without knowing Jesus as their Savior. The book of Lamentations is just that, a book of the laments or 'to mourn aloud' or to 'be sorrowful'. So, remember 3:22 and 23 from Lamentations... ***"that his mercies are new everyday"***... <u>so it's going to be a great day.</u>

3 Point Checkpoint

- ***1:09*** *Ecclesiastes* ***"What has been is what will be, and what has been done is what will be done; and there is nothing new under the sun."*** *(ESV)*
- ***2:10*** *Luke* ***"But the angel said to them, "Do not be afraid. I bring you good news that will cause great joy for all the people."*** *(NIV)*
- ***3:22*** *Lamentations* ***"The steadfast love of the Lord never ceases, his mercies never come to an end;*** [23] ***they are new every morning; great is thy faithfulness."*** *(ESV)*

*That covers the first 3 verses about his 'New Creation'... **us.** Let's make it a daily resolution to* **Take Time for God's Word** *in this week, this month and this year. I can already see what's happening in the 'new you' and I like what I see! But more importantly it is that God likes what he sees in our faithfulness, our focus, and in our repentance. So, when someone asks you, 'What's new?"... I hope that you will be able to really tell them!*

Be A New Creation *(continues)*

The 4th verse in the **New Creation** theme is from 2 Corinthians 5:17,

5:17 ***"Therefore, if anyone is in Christ, he is a new creation; the old has passed away, behold, the new has come." (ESV)***

When I read the Bible, I pay close attention to the 'tense' of the words. Some are clearly past tense describing the prior times, events, and history. Others are present tense and action oriented like, "Go", "Teach", "Baptize", or "Pray". Then there are the future tense words, those prophesying the future and speaking about end times. In this verse it starts with the present tense ***'if anyone is in Christ, he is a new creation."*** The mere fact that we can claim him as our own and repent of our sins is a 'now or immediate type of event'. We often remember the words of Jesus to the repentant thief on the cross...***"today you will be with me in paradise"***

(Luke 23:43). There is an immediacy to the Gospel... here and now.

Then it continues that ***"the old has passed away, the new has come".*** The verbs ***'has passed'*** describes a prior activity as if God knew we were coming to believe in Him (and he does). It is like kids who start getting rid of old toys before Christmas to make way for the new ones. But in this case, in our case, we are described as ***'the new'***... his new creation. When I look in the mirror, I keep hoping that more of the 'new' will start showing through and that it will take some of the wrinkles with it!

I enjoy being around my two young granddaughters because it is fun to see the world through a child's eyes. Things we take for granted are brand new to them. Watching them repeat a process over and over again just for fun and how they use the word 'WOW' multiple times in a day and are just as excited about each one is delightful. I truly pray that God would put the 'WOW' back into our lives as we again see, for the first time, his grace, his love and his mercy. When you stop to really think about it, it is a '**WOW**'! You may also have learned another **5:17** verse from 1 Thessalonians which is, ***'pray continually'*** *(NIV)*. When you are leaving work in the evening or sitting down to an early dinner, I hope that these great **5:17** verses will continue to inspire and remind you of what God has done for us and for what he is making in us each day.

Our next verse is from Jeremiah 31:31 (this one you can remember at the bottom of almost any hour (**xx:31**) of the day).

31:31 ***"Behold, the days are coming, says the LORD, when I will make a new covenant with the house of Israel and the house of Judah," (ESV).***

In order to really understand what that 'new covenant' would be, we need to read a few more verses from Jeremiah, continuing with verses 32 to 34 . It reads,

32 not like the covenant which I made with their fathers when I took them by the hand to bring them out of the land of Egypt, my cove-

nant which they broke, though I was their husband, says the LORD.

33 But this is the covenant which I will make with the house of Israel after those days, says the LORD: I will put my law within them, and I will write it upon their hearts; and I will be their God, and they shall be my people.

34 And no longer shall each man teach his neighbor and each his brother, saying, 'Know the LORD,' for they shall all know me, from the least of them to the greatest, says the LORD; for I will forgive their iniquity, and I will remember their sin no more."

I like the visualization, ***'I will write it upon their hearts.'*** It is a bit like the process that we are working through in this book to have God's Word so deeply planted in our hearts that just the 'trigger event' of a time or a visual sign is enough to repeat what we already know about God's love, his plan for our lives, and his plan for our salvation. We may not know every word of every verse but we do know the character of our God.

I also like the promise which says, ***'I will remember their sin no more.'*** Some of us would like to 'remember our sins no more' but they just keep coming up and the devil delights to have us question again and again (and again) if God could really have forgiven those past sins. When we confess, God forgives AND He does not remember those sins again. Now that is what I call a 'new covenant' or agreement. It is not something we negotiated or earned. Like all things, it was a gift from God through Christ Jesus for us. That is why we can have new hope in starting each day fresh and new in God's eyes.

Next is a verse that comes from Matthew 11:05 where we read,

11:05 ***"the blind receive their sight and the lame walk, lepers are cleansed and the deaf hear, and the dead are raised up, and the poor have good news preached to them."*** *(ESV)*

The last few words from verse 4 really start this sentence, which says, ***'Go and tell John that'***, (then starts verse 5). John had sent his disciples to ask Jesus if he is the Messiah, the one whom John spent his life proclaiming. He wanted confirmation that his words had meaning and that the 'new beginning' was found in Christ. Jesus confirmed that in our verse... new sight for the blind... new legs for the lame... new skin for the lepers... new ears for the deaf... new life for the dead... yes, even the dead got another chance when Jesus called their names. I greatly enjoy the ending, ***'and the poor have good news preached to them'.*** We talked a lot about the poor in the first theme, **Blessed**, on the Beatitudes from Matthew chapter 5:3... about the ***'poor in spirit, for theirs is the kingdom of heaven'.***

So, in these last three verses of this theme, we have 'a new covenant' that we are ***'in Christ'*** and there is ***'good news preached to them.'*** That should be both comforting and exciting to us since we all have days when we are ***'poor in spirit'***... when we don't see the hand of God as clearly as we do other days... days when the catastrophes of this world seem to overwhelm us with shock, grief, and even a bit of helplessness... what can we do? We know that we can pray... we can give... we can act... and we can hope.

Each new day bring us the chance to be that 'new creation' and to behave differently towards our family, friends and co-workers. Each new day brings the opportunity to exercise that 'new you' by digging deeper into God's word and speaking it a bit more boldly than the day before. Each new day helps us also realize that we are one day closer to eternity when there will be a ***'new heaven and a new earth'.*** Let us embrace each new year, just one day at a time, and let us experience it not just in hours and minutes but in the moments that take our breath away as we stand in awe of the power of God and in his plans for our lives.

3 POINT CHECKPOINT

- ***5:17*** *2 Corinthians* ***"Therefore, if anyone is in Christ, he is a new creation; the old has passed away, behold, the new has come." (ESV)***
- ***31:31*** *Jeremiah* ***"Behold, the days are coming, says the LORD,***

when I will make a new covenant with the house of Israel and the house of Judah," (ESV).

- ***11:05*** *Matthew* "***<u>the blind receive their sight and the lame walk,</u> lepers are cleansed and the deaf hear, and the dead are raised up, and the poor have good news preached to them."*** *(ESV)*

My goal in these short messages and in these selected verses is to help you find the one, two or 10 verses which will cause you to **<u>Take Time for God's Word</u>** *as you go about your busy days. If it can help you to change the way you act, it can also help to change the way that you think. It is to help us all realize that 'God is with us'... Immanuel.... and that makes all the difference in the world and for the world. So, be bold with that 'new creation' which is developing within you and <u>count on God to walk with you each step of the way. Make it a great week for someone you meet this week.</u>*

Be A New Creation *(continues)*

The seventh verse of the theme is from John 13:34 gives a great reminder,

13:34 ***"A new command I give you: Love one another. As I have loved you, so you must love one another." (NIV)***

This was something 'new' to the people. Jesus knew the ten commandments and the Books of the Law from his earliest days of study at the synagogue. It was therefore bold, even to the point of being like God (and that was the point) in giving people a new commandment. This was not one of the 'shalt not' commandments... those which listed the things that we cannot be part of... stealing... killing... coveting...and others. This was a commandment like the first one... "Thou shalt love the Lord thy God".... This time it is a comparison... ***"love one another. As I have loved you,..."***

It is that example of love which Jesus provided which seems to cause some people to reject Christianity. It sounds too good to be true that God, in Christ would die for us... WOW! Then for Jesus to say that we should love others in that same way... to be willing to die for them (not because we could take away their sins... Jesus already took care of that)... but to show just how deep our love is for others. We see examples of this in some people's lives... where they have 'died to self' completely and have then devoted themselves to Christian teaching, preaching, mission work or other forms of sacrificial giving and living. These people are a 'living testimony' to that new commandment. How about you??? Do others see that 'new commandment' coming through in your actions and in your living?

There is a story about a woman (or a man, take your pick) at a stop light and the driver in the car in front of her didn't see the light change or had some problem getting started through the now green light. That lady behind honked, rolled down the window and really let the driver know what she thought of that slow-to-start driver. Then the light changed again to red. The honking and verbal rebukes continued. When the light finally turned green, as the second driver was pulling through the intersection, police lights began flashing. A second police car arrived. Police had their guns drawn and the impatient driver was taken down to the police station in handcuffs. After about an hour or so, the police came to the cell to release the driver saying there had been some 'misunderstanding' and 'confusion' by the arresting officer. The driver was told... "with all of the bumper stickers about your church, Christian school, God is Love, etc. on your car.... Then seeing how you reacted and what words you said to the car in front of you, the officer thought it must be a stolen car. That's why he arrested you." <u>Let us hope and pray that we are a shining example of Christ and more than just on our bumpers.</u>

Our next verse is from Proverbs 15:30,

15:30 ***"The light of the eyes rejoices the heart, and good news refreshes the bones." (ESV)***

When dating and in the early years of marriage, spouses often refer to their mates as 'the light of my life' and their eyes truly sparkle when they say it. When their husband or wife enters a room, their eyes are fixed on that person as the most important person in the house. It is sad when there are other distractions or disruptions in life when that sense begins to fade or dies out altogether. Proverbs tries to remind us whether married or single that Jesus is the true 'Light of the World' and 'His Light brings Life.' It is just as much fun to watch Christians when they are truly in a worship setting to see in their eyes that 'light' which reflects that image of what Christ has done for them.

It definitely ***'rejoices the heart'*** as the verse says when we can know... deep down... to know that Jesus loves us... and He does. It goes on to say that ***'good news refreshes the bones.'*** For many of us, at some point in our lives, we are waiting for medical test results. We are waiting to hear if that pain or swelling or other condition is more serious. In waiting, we often fear the worst and those emotional feelings further translate into more physical symptoms. Those words ***'good news'*** even in the Old Testament brought healing and health to wearied souls. Therefore, if you are a bit out of sorts, maybe you are not focused on what brings 'good news' and that is reading and listening to God speak to us through the words of Jesus. I know it takes my mind off of the aches and pains when I am really focused on His word.

The final verse in this theme on **New Creation** comes from Psalms 51:10,

51:10 ***"Create in me a clean heart, O God, and put a new and right spirit within me." (ESV)***

That should be an easy one to remember as it is part of many church's offertory response most weeks. The numbering of the verse doesn't quite lend itself to the hours: minutes on the clock which is what often triggers a 'reminder'. But as God is not bound by time, we can link this verse to other things around us to make it more memorable. For all the football fans watching the Super Bowl or other college or NFL game, maybe you could link it to any play which goes past the 50 yard line, 1st and 10... which would be **51:10**... then do an 'instant replay' of the verse in your mind. If your favorite team is losing, this could be a GREAT reminder as you will want to take your mind off the game...and this verse is much better than any of the commercials which companies will come up with this year. We talked earlier about the heart and now we want that ***'clean heart'***. We ask for a ***'new and right spirit'*** as we begin again. It reminds us of the previous verses about the 'new covenant' and the 'new creation' which God is working in and through us. A change from the old to the new sounds like a great way to begin a new decade, a new year, or just a new day.

THREE POINT CHECKPOINT

- ***13:34** John "A new command I give you: Love one another. As I have loved you, so you must love one another." (NIV)*
- ***15:30** Proverbs "The light of the eyes rejoices the heart, and good news refreshes the bones." (ESV)*
- ***51:10** Psalms "Create in me a clean heart, O God, and put a new and right spirit within me." (ESV)*

*Whether you are at the end of a month or in a new year, we have taken a more serious look at what it means to be 'new' in the sight of God. My prayer for you is that a few times this week that you can **"Take Time for God's Word"** to thank him for that 'clean heart' and that you can be open to that 'new and right spirit' entering your life. Make this a great week as the 'new you' shows through to a world in great need.*

BE A NEW CREATION – SUMMARY

Time	Book	Verse
1:09	Ecclesiastes	***"What has been is what will be, and what has been done is what will be done; and there is nothing new under the sun." (ESV)***
2:10	Luke	***"But the angel said to them, "Do not be afraid. I bring you good news that will cause great joy for all the people." (NIV)***

Time	Book	Verse
3:22	**Lamentations**	***“The steadfast love of the Lord never ceases, his mercies never come to an end;*** [23] ***they are new every morning; great is thy faithfulness.” (ESV)***
5:17	**2 Corinthians**	***“Therefore, if anyone is in Christ, he is a new creation; the old has passed away, behold, the new has come.” (ESV)***
31:31	**Jeremiah**	***“Behold, the days are coming, says the LORD, when I will make a new covenant with the house of Israel and the house of Judah,” (ESV).***
11:05	**Matthew**	***“the blind receive their sight and the lame walk, lepers are cleansed and the deaf hear, and the dead are raised up, and the poor have good news preached to them.” (ESV)***
13:34	**John**	***“A new command I give you: Love one another. As I have loved you, so you must love one another.” (NIV)***
15:30	**Proverbs**	***“The light of the eyes rejoices the heart, and good news refreshes the bones.” (ESV)***
51:10	**Psalm**	***“Create in me a clean heart, O God, and put a new and right spirit within me.” (ESV)***

CHAPTER 6

Do What's Right

We just completed the theme of verses on the **New Creation** in you. This theme is focused on the word **Right** and in doing what is right. The 12 verses are positioned around the hours of the clock (See Resources for website/links where you can go to print this for ongoing reference). This image and focus is consistent with the process of relating time to verses and to this book **Take Time for God's Word**.

Now, my question to you is, "what does 'right' mean to you?" Who gets to decide what is "right"? In school, we are often given quizzes or tests where the teacher is looking for the "right" answers. We get graded for being "right." These scores will determine whether we get promoted to the next class; too many wrong answers and we are kept back another year until we can learn and repeat more "right" answers. Then, after we get out of school, it seems that everyone is so smart, that they can now make up their own answers regardless of the questions so that they will always be "right."

At least that's my impression of the world today. It seems to be politically incorrect to say that you are wrong... and then to be able to back it up with real facts... real truth.... real answers. In our attempts to compromise and to show tolerance, we somehow give equal weight to 'any answer' without focusing on getting to the 'right answer'. We will get to a verse in this theme which encourages us to ***'not grow weary in doing what's right'***. I believe that pausing throughout the day to remember God's word is one of those '***right***' things to do, and I am glad that you are reading this book (and getting this far into it) to help practice that process.

The first verse in our theme in this chapter is from Philippians 1:06.

1:06 ***"I am confident of this, that the one who began a good work among you will bring it to completion by the day of Jesus Christ." (NRSV)***

We all like to be around confident people, not boastful or cocky, just confident individuals. We especially like people in leadership positions to be confident so that we can rally around them. It is not very reassuring to be on a long hike into a forest only to have the guide say, "Well, I am not quite sure which way we need to go to get back to the camp. I am sure that eventually we will find it." About that time, everyone is reaching for their cell phones or checking their GPS or Google Maps™, ...if they can get a signal. No, that would not build confidence!

Here Paul is speaking to the Philippians in the first part of his letter. He wants them to know that what they had experienced when he was with them was not just 'good feelings' or 'temporary.' Paul wants them to know, with his same confidence, that the work that Jesus started in their hearts was only the beginning. That whatever 'right living' they were now seeing in their group was a result of people truly following after the heart of God. Though Paul was not with them, he wanted them to know that now the Holy Spirit was with them and that he would remain with them until the very end... ***"the day of Jesus Christ"*** as he puts it. We too need to have that same confident attitude each day as we try to live out that same 'good work'... that salvation by grace through faith... in our lives. Now that is a real confidence builder towards being on the right path.

Our second verse is also from Philippians in 2:04.

2:04 ***"Let each of you look not to your own interests, but to the interests of others." (NRSV)***

As the world news continues to bring into our living rooms the traumatic and tragic scenes from the rescue efforts from hurricanes, floods, storms, tornados, etc., this verse comes quickly to mind. It is always touching to see the outpouring of aid, food, clothes, and more sent from the US and other countries to poorer nations and victims of disasters in their time of desperate need. I am impressed by the thousands of people who go into those countries or areas to provide some of the basic needs to the people there. I am even more impressed by the thousands of missionaries and outreach teams who were there for years before the devastation working with the people to give them a glimpse of what God had planned for their salvation through Christ. I am shocked that network television crews and TV stations which will not have anything to do with mentioning the name of Jesus during 'normal times', will frequently show people praying and will talk to pastors, nurses, or missionaries about why people are praying and what benefit that has for them and those around them.

In the days following our own 9/11 disaster, (which in terms of death toll, may be less significant than earthquakes or other natural disasters,) it became acceptable to pray in public and call on God for His protection and healing at that time. For those of us as Christians, we see the devastation of sin on the world around us every day... killing people, breaking up homes, causing wars, and leading people away from the theme of our verse. It is a 'me, my, and mine' kind of world. It seems that it takes a catastrophe of epic proportions just to get people's attention. But after the cameras are gone, after the dead are buried and many forgotten, then, even more than now, we need to remember this verse (repeat it) and we need to live it so that others see God at work... just as He always has been and always will be. As we saw in Chapter 6 *"...and renew a right spirit within me."*

Our 3rd verse is from Luke 3:11.

3:11 ***"In reply he said to them, "Whoever has two coats must share with anyone who has none; and whoever has food must do likewise." (NRSV)***

When people are looking for new houses today, MORE closet space is almost always at the top of their 'must have' lists. In this country, we seem to be of the mindset that we must fill every extra inch of closet space with more clothes and 'stuff.' When they get too full, we buy special closet organizers so that we can fit everything in tighter and make a little extra room for more. When the closets again become full, we have a garage sale to get rid of the stuff that's really old so we can again buy more to fill it up.

Contrast this to what John the Baptist is asking the people to do. He is basically saying that you should share the most basic things you have with those who have NONE. Most people in his day only had two or possibly three sets of clothing. In essence, he is saying, give up one-half or one third of what you have to those in need. For most of us, that would be a lot! (but think of the closet space that would free up)! Later, when Jesus was asked a similar question about it, he said, ***"...If someone takes your coat, do not withhold your shirt from them."*** (Luke 6:29b (NIV)). He went so far as to say that when it comes to 'stuff,' we don't need much, but we do need Him.

I have to say that when I hear about the number of tons of food which our church (Trinityroselle.com) shares back with the community at the Clinics (i.e. community outreach events) that we hold, or for the holiday meal boxes and baskets we pack, I am humbled to be part of this church. I am delighted to be worshipping with so many others who 'share from the heart' this very message which John explained to the people to get them into the mindset as they needed to hear the 'good news' from Jesus. I pray that churches across the country and around the world will continue to demonstrate that they practice what Jesus teaches in very practical ways... through clothing... with food... giving shelter... offering prayers... and so much more. Again, as our pastor showed us that our Bible Study is not 'just to memorize scripture'... it is about Life... and showing that Life in Jesus to the people around us who see how we live our lives in our homes, families, and communities. For some, seeing may be their first step towards believing... ***'let us not grow weary in doing good'***....because the world is watching and is desperately in need.

Three Point Checkpoint

- ***1:06*** *Philippians* ***"I am confident of this, that the one who began a good work among you will bring it to completion by the day of Jesus Christ." (NRSV)***
- ***2:04*** *Philippians* ***"Let each of you look not to your own interests, but to the interests of others." (NRSV)***
- ***3:11*** *Luke* ***"In reply he said to them, "Whoever has two coats must share with anyone who has none; and whoever has food must do likewise." (NRSV)***

We will continue to work from the 'clock' format for the theme and I encourage you to review, to learn, and to make these verses a part of your lives as we continue to ***Take Time for God's Word****. Feel free to print extra copies or to copy the .pdf from the website (www.taketimeforgodsword.com) to send to others. I hope that this is not just my outreach to you but that this becomes 'our' outreach beyond the walls of any church and into the hearts of God's people.*

Do What's Right *(continues)*

Our 4th verse for this theme is from Philippians 4:06,

4:06 ***"Do not worry about anything, but in everything by prayer and supplication with thanksgiving let your requests be made known to God." (NRSV)***

Many years ago, a popular song was "Don't Worry, Be Happy" by Bobby McFerrin. There wasn't much more to the song than those four words and it came and it went. That seems to be the message from the world around us, 'just be happy' by whatever means it takes because 'happiness is all that there is'. Which is why so many people are miserable just trying to be happy! As we know, there is much more to our lives, as this verse states. For us, if we know Christ as our savior and we know that God is in control, then we really don't need to worry about anything (but God knows that we do worry)... so He goes even further to tell us what to do in those times... ***'in EVERYTHING by prayer and supplication with thanksgiving'*** (emphasis in mine) we are to go to God and to let our requests be known to Him.

Did God know our needs before we asked... YES! Did we need to at last humble ourselves when we finally figured out we could not fix it ourselves and our worries kept us up at night... YES! So, will we ever do that again ...most probably. Will God then hear our prayers the next time and the next and the next... most definitely! Finally, at some point, we will remember this verse... that before we hit the 'worry portion' of any situation, we will reach out and share it with God.

Then, we need to listen for his response. Some will say they have been listening for 10 minutes... 10 months... 10 years... or more. God is not slow to act based on His time schedule... but maybe on ours, it can't come soon enough. I still like the verse from Jonah 2:09 (***"But I with the voice of thanksgiving will sacrifice to thee; what I have vowed I will pay. Deliverance belongs to the LORD!"),*** when before he was thrown up by the great fish, he was already giving thanks to God. After three days inside that fish, I would think that he had something to worry about... but he knew God. Jonah knew what he had done wrong and that God was going to make it right.

I grew up in the 50's and 60's' so reading a *MAD*TM magazine once in a while was a fun activity, especially with Alfred E. Newman and his "What, me worry?" attitude. I have continued that attitude (but not the reading of *MAD* magazine) because just as Paul found, if we can grow deeper into

God's word, we will find the hope and joy and peace that we need to see us through those tough times. So, as there is often great anxiety for some people leading up to April 15th (tax deadline), we should all make this a regular verse instead of the worries about taxes and those nagging questions in your mind like... did I remember all the forms?... did I write down enough?... did I write down too much? God always gives from His abundance, even though we are working under a great deficit... and I am not talking about the national debt.

Our next verse is from Ephesians 5:08, which states,

5:08 ***"For once you were darkness, but now in the Lord you are light. Live as children of light." (NRSV)***

The sign on the side door leading to our High School photography lab and dark room said, "Don't open this door, or you will let all the dark out". (That still strikes me as funny.) This verse is very clear in its translation which says, ***'for once you were darkness'***... it does not say we were in darkness... it points directly at our hearts and says we ***'were darkness'***... (And as we know darkness is the absence of light... zero... none... nada... zilch... you get the picture).

It then immediately says, ***'now in the Lord you are light'***... again not in the light but ***'you are light'***. It is hard to hold in light... it reflects off of others... while it doesn't bend (at least not much)... it does bounce off other objects and diffuses to them. Light needs energy to keep it going... so Christ is that source of unending energy to be light through us. Some of us can relate to days where that light is just barely a flicker and other days when it is burning bright like the Sun.

The final five words of the verse are, ***"Live as children of light."*** We need to take that sentence very seriously. How are you doing in your daily living as ***'children of light'***? Does it reflect off of those who are around you? Do people 'clean up their language' when you are in the room? Do they act more respectful to you than to others? Is there some clear difference that they can see in how you live and how you treat them and others which shows the 'light' that you are?? If not yet, then how about starting this week. Make it a point of remember the verse BUT most importantly, remember how we are to live… as light. While people often do their worst deeds in physical darkness, we need to show them a better way by being children of light. I like the acronym for the new flashlights… the LED kind… as we were "led" from darkness into light, may we be those bright flashlights which do the same for others.

Our 6th verse is the theme verse from Galatians 6:09.

6:09 ***"So let us not grow weary in doing what is right, for we will reap at harvest time, if we do not give up." (NRSV)***

When I was a Program Director for 3 summers at a Lutheran Bible Camp in Iowa (www.riversidelbc.org), I used the *The Living Bible*™ as it was more contemporary as we were working with younger kids at the time. In that translation, the first part of this verse is similar but I like the added descriptors at the end. It says, ***"And let us not get tired of doing what is right, for after a while we will reap a harvest of blessings if we don't get discouraged and give up." (TLB)*** (underscore emphasis is mine).

Growing up in rural central Iowa, we knew when it was harvest time. The soy beans would turn a light tan to medium brown when the large combines would clear the fields. For the corn, it was about a month later when the huge combines with the corn picking attachments would make their ways up and down the fields from early morning until late at night to cut down those tall, tan stalks and to bring in those large ears of golden yellow corn. I like the words which describe that we will ***'reap a harvest of blessings'***.

I still remember that corn being piled high in the trailers and often overflowing to the ground, as I think of a harvest of blessings. How many of you when you were reading to your children when they were very young…. or playing ball with them… or saying bedtime prayers with and for them, ever really thought about the ***'harvest of blessing'*** that you would someday reap. For some, those blessings are yet to be realized… as the verse says ***"if we don't give up"***. For some, that is very hard. The pains are great and the times have past.... But it says, ***"if we don't give up".*** There are some who can't figure out "where we went wrong in bringing them up" and while that question still lingers, we need to repeat, ***"if we don't give up".***

If we believe that God is all powerful, then we know He is in control. While He doesn't truly need our help, he does still need our prayers so that He can know what is most important on our hearts and He hears and answers them, too. So, if you have just one verse to add to your memory banks from this theme, this one may be the one for you. In case you want to repeat it now, here it is, ***"So let us not grow weary in doing what is right, for we will reap at harvest time, if we do not give up." (NRSV)***

3 Point Checkpoint

- ***4:06*** *Philippians* ***"<u>Do not worry about anything,</u> but in everything by prayer and supplication with thanksgiving let your requests be made known to God." (NRSV)***
- ***5:08*** *Ephesians* ***"<u>For once you were darkness, but now in the Lord you are light.</u> Live as children of light." (NRSV)***
- ***6:09*** *Galatians* ***"<u>So let us not grow weary in doing what is right,</u> for we will reap at harvest time, if we do not give up." (NRSV)***

*Three verses. Common issues for all of us...**worry...darkness...giving up.** All areas which touch the heart of God in His compassion for us. He is there. He has the answer. We need to continue to be open to His teaching and listening for His guidance as we practice His Word in our daily living. <u>Make that your focus today... and every day... forever!</u>*

Do What's Right *(continues)*

Our next verse is from 2 Chronicles 7:14.

7:14 ***"if my people who are called by my name humble themselves, pray, seek my face, and turn from their wicked ways, then I will hear from heaven, and will forgive their sin and heal their land." (NRSV)***

Michael Card, a Christian singer/ songwriter, made this verse popular by arranging a song which had this verse as the key theme. He sang it for the National Day of Prayer gathering in Washington, D.C. shortly after the 9/11 tragedy. It received wide-spread notice and churches, groups, and individuals quickly saw how that song and this call from 2 Chronicles related to people today as well as to those more than 2000 years ago.

It is sad to see the number of times in the Bible and even in our own times where the people of God had forgotten their promises and had been following their own ways when tragedy struck. It is a real 'wake-up call'... like the small earthquake that happened here in Illinois. (How many people here felt it? I did not... but then I was 1846 miles away in California where the threat of earthquakes is more like a weather forecast... it is coming, we just don't know which parts will feel it the most). We know that God is in control and He deserves our respect and our thanks for the countless blessings we do receive.

In our world, too often, people will only look at the tragedies and say, 'if there was a loving God, He would not let this kind of thing happen'... as if they have a right to tell God how to be God. It is like the old quote from Voltaire, a famous French philosopher in the 1700's, who was no fan of Christianity, he wrote: *"If God made us in His image we have certainly returned the compliment."* While the Bible and even the Ten Commandments are very clear about who God is and how we should reverence Him, we humans seem to think that 'we know better' and we want to prove something to God. We saw this in the story of the Tower of Babel when the people wanted to build a spire up to the heavens and God determined to confuse their tongues so that they would not be so arrogant in their understanding of God. We need to continue to pray for this nation in times of peace and in times of conflict. <u>We too need to seek his face and pray that he will heal our land.</u>

As we work our way around the face of the clock, the next verse is from Romans 8:35,

8:35 ***"Who will separate us from the love of Christ? Will hardship, or distress, or persecution, or famine, or nakedness, or peril, or sword?" (NRSV)***

We may have heard this verse dozens of times in sermons and it may be that we gloss over it and how it relates to us. The words in the second part of the verse are a progression of difficulties or calamities which can overtake us, each more devastating than the last.

First, ***hardship***... that could be financial, personal, family, or others... it may not be too serious but still it impacts us.

Next, ***distress***.... When a ship is in trouble, it sends out a distress signal... it needs help... same is true for us.

Third is ***persecution***... this is not just occasional or periodic problems... this is where 'people are out to get you'...Christians around the world are facing this daily.

Then comes ***famine***... when you don't get enough food for days, it is 'hunger'... when there is no food for weeks or months for a wide range of people it is a famine.

Next is ***nakedness***... so not only is there no food, there is no clothing... no self-respect... everything has been taken from you.

Next is ***peril...*** which is any external force which potentially puts your very life in danger... again, it clearly indicates that you are not in control... and Finally, the ***sword...*** where people are coming to kill you... whether you deserve it or not... that is what they will do.

It is the first part of the verse which is key for Christians. It reminds us that NOTHING, large or small... internal or external... can ever separate us from the love of Christ. On valentine's day (in case that is today when you are reading this, don't forget!), we often see cards and reminders about how nothing can separate 'our love'... but we know, in a fallen world... no greeting card company can make that as a promise... it is only their wish for us.

An elderly neighbor of my daughter commented that her grandson was called up for his 3rd tour of duty in Iraq for 2 years... this just months after his first child was born. His wife does not have close family that she can stay with so the grandmother was taking her and the little boy (about 3 months old) in to live with her. The grandmother commented that she has been living alone for nearly 20 years, so this will be a real adjustment for everyone. There will be a physical separation from this soldier and his family... but not so with Christ. If we are His, He is in us through the Holy Spirit and we are his dwelling place. Now that is what I call 'a little bit of heaven right here on earth'.

Our next verse is from 2 Corinthians 9:08.

9:08 ***"And God is able to provide you with every blessing in abundance, so that by always having enough of everything, you may share abundantly in every good work." (NRSV)***

We have had a number of verses with this same type of message... and it never gets old... at least for me. I do need to be reminded often that the blessings I am getting are not mine to hold or hide or hoard. They are meant for me to enjoy but the greatest joys do come from giving... and the Bible is clear that ***'It is more blessed to give than to receive.'*** *(NIV)* (Acts 20:35b).

For me, I repeat Philippians 4:13 *(**'I can do all things through Christ who strengthens me'**)* frequently during the week. I most often need to remind myself that he does not say that I can do 'all things... ALL of the time'. Just as there are seasons of weather and seasons of life, there are seasons when we have more abundance than others. I liked the quotes from the late Zig Ziglar, a Christian motivational and management speaker, when he said, "I knew we did not have much when I was growing up but I knew we were not poor... because my mother always found clothes or other things to give to the "poor" each year." And another quote was, "We always had enough to eat at our house even in tough times. I know that because whenever I would ask for seconds, my mamma would say, 'no, you have had enough' ".

We continue to see an outpouring of money and aid to victims of man-made and natural disasters so I know that America still has a spirit of giving, which is good. We just need to follow it up with the kind of prayers and ongoing missionary support which those people will need for decades to come. If you have tried to count your blessings this day and you can do so without taking off your socks (to continue counting on your toes, too), then you aren't looking very hard. Be sure to thank God for each one of those blessings.

Point Checkpoint

- *7:14* *2 Chronicles* ***"if my people who are called by my name humble themselves, pray, seek my face, and turn from their wicked ways, then I will hear from heaven, and will forgive their sin and heal their land." (NRSV)***
- ***8:35*** *Romans* ***"Who will separate us from the love of Christ? Will hardship, or distress, or persecution, or famine, or nakedness, or peril, or sword?" (NRSV)***
- ***9:08*** *2 Corinthians* ***"And God is able to provide you with every blessing in abundance, so that by always having enough of everything, you may share abundantly in every good work." (NRSV)***

Think abundance this week... not in the stuff which you have but with the gifts that God has waiting to give to those who will just ask. Have a great day, in His name.

Do What's Right *(continues)*

The final 3 verses for this theme will complete the series of a verse for every hour. Keep practicing until you have several verses for each hour to choose from.

Our 10th verse is found in 1 Corinthians 10:24.

10:24 ***"Do not seek your own advantage, but that of the other." (NRSV)***

This verse is kind of the 'book ends' to the verse which you may have learned previously from Philippians 2:04, "***Let each of you look not to your own interests, but to the interests of others". (NRSV).*** So, if you are driving your car this week, and your hands are in the driving positions of 10 o'clock and 2 o'clock... then think of 1 Corinthians **10:24** and Philippians 2:04. And while the verses are similar, this verse uses the word 'advantage' and the other says 'interests'. Here are some situations where we could seek our own advantage and the world view is likely to support us on it... like:

Someone gives you too much change back on a purchase... do you take it and run .....OR return it and watch their reaction.

Someone needs to get into your lane due to a lane merger... do you ignore their signal or waving and speed on...OR slow down and let them in.

You see a parking spot and get ready to turn in... OR do you let the car that was already waiting for it have that spot as they were blocked by the car pulling out.

You've waited all week for your favorite show on TV but your spouse or a family member has their show on already ... do you grab the remote and change the channel... OR do you tape it (OR DVR or TIVO™... because no one uses tape anymore) for later viewing.

In each of these situations, the world would say... you have the rights or right of way, so take it... but our verse says otherwise. We are to seek the advantage of the other. By doing so, you will stand out from the crowd. People will stop to ask you, "why did you do that" or "what was that all about"? Then you can actually stop to tell them about this great story... how someone died in your place, not because he had to, but because he wanted to... and ever since then, you have decided to live differently because that's what he wanted for you... and he can do the same for each of them. The Gospel message is just that personal and just that simple. All we need to do is tell it.

Our next verse is from Hebrews 11:06.

11:08 ***"And without faith it is impossible to please God, for whoever would approach him must believe that he exists and that he rewards those who seek him." (NRSV)***

Two short 'real world' stories which caught my attention. From several years ago, the first was in a 5 minute cab ride in San Francisco... public radio is playing in the cab... the commentator was noticeably agitated by the Pat Robertson (TV evangelist/ host) comments about the earthquake in Haiti... as a quote he read from prior history about Haiti's involvement with the practice of Voodoo. The commentator acknowledged that he was an agnostic but made these quick comments... "if there were a loving God, He would not have let this disaster destroy so much of Haiti"...and..."if there were a God, then He, or She, or It would strike down Pat Robertson for what he said about Haiti... but because Pat is still alive, then I guess there is no God".

The second event was a headline by an atheist organization that said that they would be glad to take care of people's abandoned pets after the Rapture takes place... so people won't need to worry about them. So, here we have an agnostic who basically has no time for any God but who is upset because of what God did (i.e. the earthquake) and what God did not do (i.e. strike down Pat Robertson)... As if that person knows how to be God without believing there even is one. Then, the atheists are acknowledging a Rapture, which is the return of Christ and the end of the world, BUT they are worried more about other people's pets more than they are their own souls.

As Christians, we recognize that even faith is a gift from God and that through faith we not only believe He exists but we can know it deep within our hearts. Through that faith, even as tiny as a mustard seed, we can do great things through His love as we share it with others. I continue to ask that God will open the eyes of the spiritually blind so that they can get a peek at His glory... and I pray that they will see something of Christ in what I do and in how I live. How about you??

Our last verse for this theme on **Right** is from Romans 12:10.

12:10 ***"Love one another with mutual affection; outdo one another in showing honor." (NRSV)***

After Valentine's Day (or a birthday, anniversary, etc.) has passed and after the roses have wilted, the cards have been filed or tossed, and the chocolates are all gone (or hidden so that others can't find them), we need to remind ourselves that those one-day expressions of love are not the only ones we share throughout the year. I like the request which comes in the first part of the verse to love ***'with mutual affection'***. It is a small request but a HUGE issue in any kind of relationship. We somehow keep score (with great memories about past failures) as to who loves more than the other (and somehow our memory seems to favor our scorecard). Yet we are reminded that Paul is just sharing what he learned and saw in the other Apostles... that Christ showed the ultimate love for us, so with such a great example, a mutual love for others is just the minimum that we should be able to provide in return.

Then Paul adds the kicker to the verse... ***'outdo one another in showing honor'***. In this case, the word ***'honor'*** means 'the act of showing great respect or high regard'... in simple terms, it means putting the other person first. Therefore, in all of our actions, we are to show that we are willing to put someone's interests, or needs, or wants, or feelings, or safety, or ... and the list goes on... that showing our love is to show they are first in our lives.

We see it in healthy marriages. We see it in loving families and churches. And, we see it occasionally in ourselves, when we finally come to realize it is about putting God first in our lives. It is about making Jesus at home in our homes and in our hearts. It is about forgetting who we are and in looking deeply into the eyes and into the hearts of those around us to see what they need and how we can help them to find it... and that includes helping them to find out who Jesus is. So, this week, I encourage you to focus on these 12 short words–one for each step of your new 12 step program to begin changing your world by loving each other deeply and then taking it to the next level by showing honor to others in your life. <u>I know you will see a big difference in how you are being treated as the love of Christ will reflect on others and then come right back to you.</u>

3 Point Checkpoint

- ***10:24** 1 Corinthians **"Do not seek your own advantage, but that of the other." (NRSV)***
- ***11:06** Hebrews **"And without faith it is impossible to please God, for whoever would approach him must believe that he exists and that he rewards those who seek him.: (NRSV)***
- ***12:10** Romans **"Love one another with mutual affection; outdo one another in showing honor." (NRSV)***

We have completed this 12 verse, round-the-clock card format. We will work through another one in coming chapters where we will look at verses from chapters 13-24 as we continue to **Take Time for God's Word** *in just a few minutes per day. I find that different verses come to mind more quickly and more clearly by using this technique. I hope it is having a positive impact on you as well. I am delighted to find new verses each week to share with each of you on Facebook and on the Web as we make this journey through God's Word together. It has been an exciting journey so far with Him and I know the best is yet to come. Make it a great week in your walk with Him.*

Do What's Right – Summary

Time	Book	Verse
1:06	Philippians	***"I am confident of this, that the one who began a good work among you will bring it to completion by the day of Jesus Christ." (NRSV)***
2:04	Philippians	***"Let each of you look not to your own interests, but to the interests of others." (NRSV)***

Time	Book	Verse
3:11	Luke	*"In reply he said to them, "Whoever has two coats must share with anyone who has none; and whoever has food must do likewise." (NRSV)*
4:06	Philippians	*"Do not worry about anything, but in everything by prayer and supplication with thanksgiving let your requests be made known to God." (NRSV)*
5:08	Ephesians	*"For once you were darkness, but now in the Lord you are light. Live as children of light." (NRSV)*
6:09	Galatians	*"So let us not grow weary in doing what is right, for we will reap at harvest time, if we do not give up." (NRSV)*
7:14	2 Chronicles	*"if my people who are called by my name humble themselves, pray, seek my face, and turn from their wicked ways, then I will hear from heaven, and will forgive their sin and heal their land." (NRSV)*
8:35	Romans	*"Who will separate us from the love of Christ? Will hardship, or distress, or persecution, or famine, or nakedness, or peril, or sword?" (NRSV)*
9:08	2 Corinthians	*"And God is able to provide you with every blessing in abundance, so that by always having enough of everything, you may share abundantly in every good work." (NRSV)*
10:24	1 Corinthians	*"Do not seek your own advantage, but that of the other." (NRSV)*

Time	Book	Verse
11:06	Hebrews	*"And without faith it is impossible to please God, for whoever would approach him must believe that he exists and that he rewards those who seek him." (NRSV)*
12:10	Romans	*"Love one another with mutual affection; outdo one another in showing honor." (NRSV)*

CHAPTER 7

Watch And Pray

In the last chapter, we finished up verses drawn from the Bible books with chapters 1-12 as a series linked to the face of a clock (and a .pdf image to show those verses). This was meant to help you visualize and link verses to specific times on a clock and to think about them throughout your day. There is a similar series at www.taketimeforgodsword.com in the Samples tab with that series of verses from Chapters 13 – 24 of Matthew. Here are a few of my favorites: 13:44, 16:24, 18:20, ... Oh, you would like to know what the words are, too?? Ok, we can do that as well (just to encourage you to link to that material as well... it is free to use it).

All from the book of Matthew:

- *13:44* ***"The kingdom of heaven is like treasure hidden in a field, which a man found and covered up; then in his joy he goes and sells all that he has and buys that field." (RSV)***
- *16:24* ***Then Jesus told his disciples, "If any man would come***

after me, let him deny himself and take up his cross and follow me." (RSV)

- *18:20 "For where two or three are gathered in my name, there am I in the midst of them." (RSV)*
- *20:16 "So the last will be first, and the first last." (RSV)*
- *21:22 "And whatever you ask in prayer, you will receive, if you have faith." (RSV)*
- *24:35 "Heaven and earth will pass away, but my words will not pass away." (RSV)*

And there were more so I do hope that you can review those sometime soon to bring those verses to mind throughout your days, weeks, and years to come.

In this chapter, we are working through both the Gospels of Mark and Luke to review other key verses from those books of the Bible. There were many verses similar to those from Matthew so I did not repeat them here. The first two of the first three verses have the word **WATCH** in them so that is a focus word for us for this series. (You can see website/links in the Resources that there is a brief definition and some thoughts and quotes about what it means to **WATCH**.) If you can save that visual or print it out (see Chapter 10 for ideas on using these types of materials), then those can help you gain even more focus on the 12 verses we will cover in this chapter. We will use the Revised Standard Version (RSV) for this series of verses. My point is to give you exposure to several translations and phrasing of verses. Often, it causes you to pay more attention to the words OR makes some verses even more meaningful or relevant to your situation or needs. Just as you saw in the prior chapter, the few key words from each verse are at the top of the page by the clock are a way to test yourself on whether you can say the whole verse by just getting a few starter words. Some are short verses so the key words listed make up about ½ of the verse. With a little practice, you will have these added to your memory banks in no time... AND I know in those banks that they will get great interest there.

Our first verse for this theme is from Mark 13:33.

13:33 ***"Take heed, watch; for you do not know when the time will come." (RSV).***

This is from a part of Mark where people are asking about when the end will come. Jesus does not try to make detailed predictions as some are trying to do from the ancient Aztec's calendar or from the writings or predictions of Nostradamus. Jesus talks about what will be happening in the world which may cause people to think that the end is near, but those are just the beginning of what to watch for. Instead, he reminds his disciples, and us today, to ***"Take heed, watch".*** To **take heed**, (not commonly used term today), means to "to give careful attention to; take notice of; to mind"... (Another word we don't hear too often... **mind**... like 'mind your manners'... or 'mind your parents'...so I guess that kids these days have just lost their 'mind' or something like that... but maybe that's what our parents said about us, too?).

We are called by Jesus to give careful attention to what is going on in the world around us. Not so that we can know about the end, BUT so that we can help others learn about a new beginning. He often reminds us that time is short and our time on earth is fleeting so we dare not waste the opportunities which we have to share his word and to speak his name. So, humorously speaking, we may not know when the time will come... BUT hopefully we will have one or more verses on our minds when it does come... (you know... **Take Time for God's Word**).... Ok, moving on.

Our second verse is from Mark 14:38.

14:38 ***"Watch and pray that you may not enter into temptation; the spirit indeed is willing, but the flesh is weak." (RSV)***

Another way to think about this is a phrase I heard years ago which said, "When it is a contest between your will and your imagination, imagination will win every time" (attributed to Bob Proctor). How often do we start to dream of great and Godly things and then imagination creeps in and we have some wild dreams of fame, fortune, more happiness than we have now... that new car, and boat, or even airplane... the travels... the food... Ok, you get the picture. What started as a noble idea turned into what would be front page headlines in a tabloid paper... and we have way too many examples of that already.

Here, in our verse, Jesus is talking to his disciples, close friends who have been with him for 3 years. It is the path to crucifixion and Jesus wants their support as he begins his preparations for his death. He asks:

- ***Watch and pray***...most of us know that feeling... we wake up in the morning without ever remembering the Amen from the prayer the night before...
- ***Watch and pray....*** We start prayers for others around us but somehow end up quickly with the troubles that are on our mind and what we plan to ask God for next....
- ***Watch and pray....***we hear the news about the devastation in yet another part of the world, like in Chile with an 8.8 earthquake, one of the highest readings on record, and we kind of tune out as we have heard so much bad news from other disasters like the hurricane that hit Haiti. We just can't focus on the needs of others again so soon....
- ***Watch and pray...***For God knows our weaknesses and our frailty but he still calls us to watch and pray that we not enter into temptation.... For temptations will come... but God will always have an escape route if we are willing to look for it... ***So watch and pray.***

Next is our verse from Luke 15:10.

15:10 ***"Just so, I tell you, there is joy before the angels of God over one sinner who repents." (RSV)***

This verse is the culmination to the parable of the Lost Coin. That parable followed the one about the Lost Sheep. And the Lost Coin is just before the story of the Prodigal Son.... Another one who was lost. How many of you have ever been lost???

How many of you have ever lost a child, even for a few minutes, where you did not know where they were and you feared the worst. It happened to our family while visiting the Mall of America in the Twin Cities, Minnesota. I only heard about it second hand as I came to meet the family there at the end of a business trip. Fortunately, my wife had told the kids that if they got lost, to ask a store worker where the Lego™ display was and they would meet there. Our son was about 8 years old at the time. The family was talking with other relatives as they walked through the mall and into the center area. Our son was looking in the windows and checking out what he wanted as a souvenir when he looked up and everyone was gone. When my wife later turned and did not find him with them, she quickly notified the security... age, height, name, what he was wearing, etc...the family split up to look for him... and sure enough about 30 minutes later, one of them checked at the Lego's place and there he was playing with the blocks, just like his mom told him... if he got lost, he knew where to go to be found again.

That story sounds a bit like Jesus when he was 12... parents didn't know where he was, but he knew where he needed to go to be found. I always laugh when I pass by the signs in the parochial school area in our church which have arrows that point to the "Lost and Found" and it seems like it is pointing to the main sanctuary of the church. I think that is true. <u>That is God's meeting place each week for us, the Lost and the Found, for we know we can find him there patiently waiting for us.</u>

3 Point Checkpoint

- ***13:33*** Mark ***"<u>Take heed, watch</u>; for you do not know when the time will come." (RSV).***
- ***14:38*** Mark ***"<u>Watch and pray</u> that you may not enter into temptation; the spirit indeed is willing, but the flesh is weak." (RSV)***

- ***15:10*** Luke ***"Just so, I tell you, there is joy before the angels of God over one sinner who repents." (RSV)***

As I said earlier, I hope that you will look at the key words around the clock portion of the card on the website listed in the Resources a few times during the week as it may help you to bring to mind the verse and the meaning which God has planned in it for you. Take a moment to think about who else in your life could benefit from these same verses and then copy/ paste or print/ share it with others. His Word and the Good News of the Gospel is too great to just keep to ourselves, we need to be diligent in passing it on to others. So, I hope that you have a watch-full day and expect great blessings... not just in the getting but also in your giving of those blessings to others.

WATCH AND PRAY *(CONTINUES)*

The fourth verse is taken from Mark 16:16.

16:16 ***"He who believes and is baptized will be saved; but he who does not believe will be condemned." (RSV)***

This is from a part of Mark after Jesus is raised from the dead. The preceding verse is the 'Great Commission' as recorded by Mark. In our world, many people trying to be 'politically correct' would say that this verse is too harsh, or too divisive, or too restrictive. They would like to think that there is an asterisk or footnote someplace which gives them an 'out-clause'... one where they can 'kinda believe' but not too much. The world would say that part about being condemned, well that's just un-American to say those kinds of things. The world would say that we are not being inclusive enough for their liking. But, Jesus had just a few short days before his ascension. He needed to be very clear to his disciples. There is no time for long teaching sessions... just the basic truth and the simple message of the Gospel, ***"He who believes and is baptized will be saved; but he who does not believe will be condemned."*** Jesus knows his followers both then and now. He knows that if we try to make the message of the cross too complex, people won't remember it. We need to be able to fall back on the direct, honest, and yes, sometimes difficult messages, to share with the people around us. They need to know that his salvation is a free gift which comes to them only IF they will believe.

That is what faith is...as our pastor often shows by example; it is 'leaning upon something to support you and trusting it with all of your weight'... if it fails you, you will fall. Otherwise, it will help you to stand firm against other winds of change and pressures from all sides. If you can only remember these three words... ***He who believes***, then I think that you already know the verse, but more importantly, you know in whom we believe. That truly makes all the difference in the world.

Our next verse is from Luke 17:10.

17:10 ***"So you also, when you have done all that is commanded you, say, 'We are unworthy servants; we have only done what was our duty.'" (RSV)***

In my early years at college (ages ago), my favorite translation was the JB Phillips version of the New Testament. I attended a two-year ALC Lutheran college named Waldorf College (now Waldorf University; www.waldorf.edu), in northern Iowa, and I was part of a Lutheran Youth Encounter™ (LYE) team which would go out on weekends to help in rural church's youth meetings or even Sunday worship services. So, we would leave Friday late afternoons and get back early Sunday evenings. Those trips were exhausting but greatly rewarding to see the impact on youth groups and on individual teenagers as they heard about the Gospel from those nearly their own age. It was after one of those long weekends and getting ready for a 7:45am Monday morning Calculus class that I read these words and underlined them in my New Testament. (If you could see the book's condition, well-worn with tape holding it together, tattered pages, heavily marked up, you would know that it when through A LOT those early years). It phrased this verse as, ***"we are not much good as servants, for we have only done what we ought to do"***. It was at that point that

I realized that we should always be giving our 110% effort for God. That what seemed like doing so much for him was just what I should be doing.

I know that most of us as parents have been asked by our kids… 'what have you done for me lately', as they think that they are becoming independent and that mom and dad may not seem as important as they once were. If you are like me, I am ready with a whole LONG list of items, in alphabetical order, of ALL that we have done for them that they will never even notice or even care about until later in their lives. And that must be a bit of how God must feel for us (without the long list, I am sure). All the countless blessings, both seen and unseen, which he has poured out upon us and when we do something little for him, we somehow think we deserve recognition. ***"So you also, when you have done all that is commanded you, say, 'We are unworthy servants; we have only done what was our duty.'"*** <u>So, let's keep on doing what we ought to do…then seeing where we can do even more.</u>

The sixth verse in the theme **Watch** is from Luke 18:41.

18:41 ***"What do you want me to do for you?" He said, "Lord, let me receive my sight." (RSV)***

This verse is near the end of Chapter 18 as Jesus is on his way to Jericho. In this story, the blind beggar hears the crowds passing by and hears that Jesus is with them. He cries out Jesus' name to have pity on him… others tell him to be quiet, but the man persists. Finally, Jesus stops and asks the man this question, ***"What do you want me to do for you?"*** For a blind man, maybe the answer seems obvious. In another translation, it says, ***"Lord, make me see again."*** (*J B Phillips Translation*) That would imply that he had lost his sight at some point, but that he knew what it was like to have sight. If any of you have been sight impaired, even for a few hours, you do know just how much we take for granted when we can see the world around us and when we aren't walking in darkness.

So, let's take it to a more personal level. If Jesus were standing there in front of you today asking that same question of you, ***"What do you want***

me to do for you?"... what would your request be?? Physical healing of some kind... Healing of a relationship or getting a family back together... spiritual healing... Or something else? You really don't need to imagine it. Jesus is just that close to you right now and every minute of the day. He does want to know what he can do for you and for your loved ones. He cares deeply about you and knows your every need, even the ones which we are too ashamed or proud to ask for on our own.

I hope and pray that each morning when you first open your eyes and get that first glimpse of another new day full of grace, that you will repeat with that blind man, ***"Lord, let me receive my sight"......*** let me see the world as you see it. Let me see the needs and the opportunities and the people who need your love through me this day. The verse is Luke **18:41**. So, while **18:41** is really **6:41** ***pm***, you can associate great verses with any time or activity throughout your day. Maybe you want to tape those numbers to your clock as a reminder to see the world through the love of Christ this week.

3 Point Checkpoint

- ***16:16*** *Mark* ***"He who believes and is baptized will be saved; but he who does not believe will be condemned." (RSV)***
- ***17:10*** *Luke* ***"So you also, when you have done all that is commanded you, say, 'We are unworthy servants; we have only done what was our duty.'" (RSV)***
- ***18:41*** *Luke* ***"What do you want me to do for you?" He said, "Lord, let me receive my sight." (RSV)***

We have now covered ½ the verses in chapters 13-24 as we continue to **Take Time for God's Word.** *How well do you remember them? For some reading this, Easter week will be coming soon, so I do hope that we can pause during this Lenten season (or at any time) to listen to God's call to us through His word. This is often a time when people are more receptive to hearing about the Good News about the Cross and the empty tomb.*

WATCH AND PRAY *(CONTINUES)*

Our 7th verse in this chapter is from Luke 19:40.

19:40 ***"He answered, "I tell you, if these were silent, the very stones would cry out." (RSV)***

This verse was Jesus reply to the Pharisees when they asked him to quiet the people from singing their hallelujahs and rejoicing at his entry into Jerusalem. It's hard for us in urban America to get the image here. I was in Jerusalem in the early 1970's and I am sure it is much the same today. The narrow passageways through the city are cobblestone. They show the wearing down from nearly 2000 years of use and millions of people who have walked those paths. The walls of the city are stone-upon-stone. There are narrow steps and passageways to the top of the walls where watchmen could see who was approaching and could let the people know in advance to prepare for this coming King.

The imagery then and now remains the same. That is, when Christ comes in his glory, whether 2000 years ago or in the next minutes or the next millennium, that entrance deserves the recognition and attention of all the people. If the people cannot or will not give that recognition, then even creation itself, down to the very rocks and stones around us will give testimony to the King of Kings. Let us not miss our chance on Palm Sunday (and everyday) to give him the recognition and praise which he deserves.... And let's not take it for granite... er, granted.

Our next verse is from Luke 20:25,

20:25 ***"He said to them, "Then render to Caesar the things that are Caesar's, and to God the things that are God's." (RSV)***

On the trip to the Holy Land in 1973, we stopped at Masada in southern Israel not far from the Dead Sea. It was a last Jewish stronghold which would not surrender to Roman invaders. The Romans encamped around it for many months and finally they carried tons of rock and dirt to build a ramp up the side of the plateau to enter into the camp. The Jews inside vowed not to be captured and chose 10 men to kill the more than 900 members of the camp then 1 of them would kill the 9 and then himself. And, you are probably asking what this story has to do with our verse? Great question... here's the transition.

While we were at the top of Masada seeing the excavations, mosaics, etc. a worker from the excavation asked some of us if we were interested in coins dug up from that site. They were caked over with dirt and clay but we could see that they were real. We bought a small bag of them ....30 or so, for about $25. I had given some of the better pieces to family members as their souvenirs but I have included photos on the website of some of the coins. In these photos, you will see some small 'widow's mite' coins... and a few which bear the likeness of a Caesar. So, when Jesus asked for a coin, it was plain to see who it was paying tribute to.

His response is just as plain to us today. We are to be stewards of His blessings and that we may we use them for his kingdom's sake. Maybe 50 or 100 or 150 years from now people will be describing the great actions, sacrifices, and dedication of you who are reading this book... just as the Jews retell the story of Masada from generation to generation. May those blessings be the memories that get retold... and not some worn pieces of metal with faces of people long gone and forgotten. So, as you handle coins in your pocket or purse today, remember this verse. It will be a 'change' that can stay with you the rest of your life.

Verse 9 for our theme is from Luke 21:13.

21:13 *"This will be a time for you to bear testimony." (RSV)*

This is a short verse. One which you can likely recall with very little practice. (Repeat it now and you will have it memorized.) It is also one of the hardest verses for Christians through the ages. It is hard because it is a personal challenge to each of us. It is a challenge for us to be the 'I witnesses' and 'eye-witnesses'. Have any of you been a witness at a court hearing or a trial??

For more than 200 years, the tradition was that a witness needed to be 'sworn in' before giving their testimony. They were asked to put their left hand on the Bible and with their right hand uplifted to swear to 'tell the truth, the whole truth, and nothing but the truth, so help me God." There was a public recognition that God was a higher authority than the courts and that God knows the Truth and that He would punish those who strayed from telling it clearly. Today, there may be a 'swearing in' but rarely is a Bible used. For some, it is bring your own book, like the Koran, and you can be sworn in based on that faith. Most often, it is just based on personal word or the expectation of integrity when testifying in a court... and which can provide its own forms of punishment if the person is found to be lying.

In the movie, "*Fried Green Tomatoes*", a young woman was on trial and the lawyers for the plaintiff were trying to establish her whereabouts at a given time. Her local minister took the stand to testify on her behalf. When offered a Bible to be sworn in upon, he replied that he brought his own 'good book'. His testimony was considered credible and the woman was cleared of all charges. She knew his testimony saved her but asked how he could have said things that were not true. He confided in her that the 'good book' which he was sworn in upon was his favorite copy of *Moby Dick*. He said that only seemed appropriate for the 'whale-of-a-tale' which he told... And he reminded her to not miss the Sunday meeting where all sins can be forgiven. So, with the ever increasing pressure for a separation of 'church and state', this truly is our time to give a testimony to who we are and whose we are. Let's be willing to share both the truth of the Gospel and the Good News of the Gospel to a world that is losing its moral bearings and its sense of true justice.

3 POINT CHECKPOINT

- ***19:40** Luke* ***"He answered, "I tell you, if these were silent, the very stones would cry out." (RSV)***
- ***20:25** Luke* ***"He said to them, "Then render to Caesar the things that are Caesar's, and to God the things that are God's." (RSV)***

- ***21:13** Luke **"This will be a time for you to bear testimony." (RSV)***

Reminder: When someone asks you 'What time is it?' answer it and then add... that your day seems to go much better when you **Take Time for God's Word**. *Ask if they would want to give it a try. You just may be surprised at their response. Share the links on the Web (www.taketimeforgodsword.com) or on Facebook (www.facebook.com/taketimeforgodsword). They may be eternally grateful that you were willing to share the Good News with them! Try it!*

Watch And Pray *(continues)*

Our next verse is from Luke 22:27 which reads,

> 22:27 ***"For which is the greater, one who sits at table, or one who serves? Is it not the one who sits at table? But I am among you as one who serves."***

For many of us, we enjoy going out to our favorite restaurant (no, not through the drive through lane). We like to sit down and have people take our order and deliver our food. We pay extra (through tips) for great service. It makes us feel special. For some of us, we have memories of being on the other side of the story. We were the waitress or waiter, the busboy, or cook or cleanup/ dishwasher crew. Our memories may be of rude people that we just could not please OR of people dressed fancy and 'rich' who left a crummy tip (if they left a tip at all). So much for our human experiences. Let's reframe our thinking a bit here.

Jesus continues to impress upon his disciples that seeing the world through its vision puts people in roles of service as someone in a lesser role or position. Jesus reminds them (and us) that to be in a position of service to others is really one of the greatest roles we can have. That is what Jesus came to earth to provide. That is what we are called upon to also provide to others. It is not for our sake but for the sake of the Gospel that we offer up such service to others.

Some of our greatest leaders are those who know the role and responsibilities to which they have been called or elected BUT they know that unless they can show a level of servant-leadership, that they will have lost the confidence and support from most of their followers. That means they are looking out for the interests of others. They are anticipating needs. They are preparing for those needs in advance. They are there when the need arises. AND, they often provide such service so well that many people/ most people will not even realize that it happened. What they needed was 'just there'.

That is what Christ does for us. He knows our needs. He is prepared to meet those needs. He often provides blessings which we did not even know we needed but they came anyway. So, how can you be a better servant today? Whose needs can your fulfill, even without them knowing about it? How can you let God get the glory for your quiet acts of kindness and love shown to others? Let that be your goal today... and every day. The world will start to notice. It does make a difference. It did for Jesus and He will make it have impact for you as well. Go and serve the Lord!

Moving on to Luke for another verse, let's read from Luke 23:34,

23:34 ***And Jesus said, "Father, forgive them; for they know not what they do."***

These were Jesus words from the Cross to the mob who had gathered there. Some came to jeer. Others came to cry. And still others came just there to see what was going on. What would have been your reaction? What is your reaction today??

I have often thought about what it means to be an 'average sinner'. In school that may be 'C' student (while with 'grade inflation' that is likely moving up to a 'B' these days... after all, no one likes to be thought of as just average anymore). But the "C+" sinner is the one who delights in or who at least acknowledges the 'commission of sins'... doing things then being sorry for them. Therefore, the 'commission' has the 'c' included in the word so that becomes the '+' in the C+. The "C-" sinner is the one who may specialize (if that is the right way to look at it) in the 'sins of omission' ... who doesn't do things that should have been done and then worries about them. For many people, they are likely to be oblivious to those sins as they just aren't even on their radar that they did anything in the situation that could be considered as wrong. That was probably like many of the people who witnessed the crucifixion. Now you can remember the differences between the Commission (C+) or Omission (C-).

I guess maybe we should model ourselves after the Apostle Paul who claims to the 'the greatest of sinners' (maybe he was an A+ sinner). Or maybe we just continue to cling to the grace and mercy that God gave us through Christ's death and through his words (repeat the verse). So, do what you know is right to do... AND watch for those situations where you may be tempted to 'do nothing' but test it to see if you should be proactive in making a situation better by getting involved.

Our final verse in the series is from Luke 24:48, (and I know that for those people who use the 24 hour clock and who may operate on military time, that this would be 00:48 BUT as there are no '00' chapters in the Bible, we will use '24' as the reference. That should make it even more memorable for you... it goes beyond time!)

24:48 *"You are witnesses of these things." (RSV)*

Just six words but a very powerful statement. If you have seen a crime or an accident, you may have been called upon to be a witness to that incident. People want to know what you saw, heard, experienced, etc. They want an account from someone who was actually there. They want it first-hand. AND they want it to be truthful and accurate.

So, while we were not there with Jesus more than 2000 years ago, we do have the written words of those who were witnesses to all that He said and did. We have it from multiple disciples / authors. We have had it reviewed by multiple organizations through the ages. While they have agreed with the testimony given, it now comes down to you. Are you able to be a witness to what you have seen, heard, and experienced in your own life due to the Good News about Jesus Christ? Then comes the question, "Will you?"

Each of us is called to be a faithful to tell others of what Christ has done for us. It is as simple (and sometimes challenging) as that... tell others what we have experienced in Christ. Can you do that today? Will you do that whenever someone asks? Have the confidence and the conviction to state what you know by faith to be true. You will be blessed by doing it AND you will be a blessing to others. Sharing the Good News and inviting others to come to know Christ is a great privilege and responsibility. Try it. Practice it. Do it for the sake of the Gospel. Well Done!

3 Point Checkpoint

- ***22:27** Luke "For which is the greater, one who sits at table, or one who serves? Is it not the one who sits at table? But I am among you as one who serves." (RSV)*
- ***23:34** Luke And Jesus said, "Father, forgive them; for they know not what they do." (RSV)*
- ***24:48** Luke "You are witnesses of these things." (RSV)*

We are reminded of greater ***service****...great* ***forgiveness****... great* ***opportunities to witness*** *to others. Luke adds a personal and insightful view to what Christ said and did in His short time on earth. We can learn a lot from that perspective. To live life with emotion and empathy for others is a great calling for each of us. I do pray that these verses become much more than just 'memory' verses. I pray that these become 'life' verses on how you think... how you act... how you respond...and how you live. We are called to live life to the full in Christ and knowing His Word deeply will help each of us to accomplish that mission.*

Summary – Watch and Pray

Time	Book	Verse
13:33	Mark	*"Take heed, watch; for you do not know when the time will come." (RSV).*
14:38	Mark	*"Watch and pray that you may not enter into temptation; the spirit indeed is willing, but the flesh is weak." (RSV)*
15:10	Luke	*"Just so, I tell you, there is joy before the angels of God over one sinner who repents." (RSV)*
16:16	Mark	*"He who believes and is baptized will be saved; but he who does not believe will be condemned." (RSV)*
17:10	Luke	*"So you also, when you have done all that is commanded you, say, 'We are unworthy servants; we have only done what was our duty.'" (RSV)*
18:41	Luke	*"What do you want me to do for you?" He said, "Lord, let me receive my sight." (RSV)*
19:40	Luke	*"He answered, "I tell you, if these were silent, the very stones would cry out." (RSV)*
20:25	Luke	*"He said to them, "Then render to Caesar the things that are Caesar's, and to God the things that are God's." (RSV)*
21:13	Luke	*"This will be a time for you to bear testimony." (RSV)*
22:27	Luke	*"For which is the greater, one who sits at table, or one who serves? Is it not the one who sits at table? But I am among you as one who serves." (RSV)*

Time	Book	Verse
23:34	Luke	***And Jesus said, "Father, forgive them;*** ***for they know not what they do." (RSV)***
24:48	Luke	***"You are witnesses of these things." (RSV)***

CHAPTER 8

Know the I AM

This series looks at a few of the key verses which have the "I AM" references in them. These are important as they establish the sovereignty of God… there is NONE higher than He. He is the Creator, Redeemer, and ultimately the final Judge over this world. Yet, we can have a personal relationship with Him through Jesus. I enjoy the Christian chorus which says, "I am a friend of God…He knows my name." Now that is a LONG term relationship that we can enjoy forever. Take a few minutes every day to be reminded of who God is and that you can have a personal and lasting relationship with Him. Know the great I AM verses but more importantly, know the I AM Savior of your life!

The first verse comes from Exodus 3:14 and it states,

3:14 ***God said to Moses, "I AM WHO I AM. This is what you are to say to the Israelites: 'I AM has sent me to you.'" (NIV)***

We all want to feel important. We all want to have significance in what we do. We want to align ourselves with those who have power and authority. That is what Moses was doing. He had a powerful message to give his people. It would change their lives and their fate. He knew it. But, he knew that they would not believe it if it were just coming from himself. He needed to speak with a voice of authority. He asked God for help (good plan!). Here is where God speaks that statement "I AM WHO I AM". We often find that there aren't enough words to really describe God. So, we find that it is condensed down to the most simple and basic of statements. I AM. The constant presence of a being. Always here. Always personal. Always with us. Always and forever the same. That's our God. It is why knowing Him and knowing Jesus as Savior and friend makes all the difference in the world. Once Moses knew that he had that kind of support and that kind of 'references' when speaking to the people, he went on to carry the message to his people and even to the Pharaoh himself. While Moses still had some self-doubts, he did not doubt that God was with Him and that God would provide a way to set his people free. God still wants that for each of us. To be free from sin. To make an exodus from our old life and old self. To make the journey with Him through every new day and every new adventure yet to come in our lives. Don't miss out. Take that journey. Follow the great I AM and you will have the time of your life (like **3:14**).

Our next verse jumps ahead hundreds of years but it still has that same immediacy to it as we consider 41:10 Isaiah,

41:10 ***Don't be afraid, for I am with you. Don't be discouraged, for I am your God. I will strengthen you and help you. I will hold you up with my victorious right hand. (NLT)***

Fear. It comes in all shapes, sizes, times, places, etc. For some people it is constant. For others it comes and goes BUT when it is present, it is or can be all consuming. Most often, it is not rational. It is not even real. That does not stop us from focusing on it and letting it paralyze our thinking and stop our actions. It is that powerful. That is why this verse is so critical to know and to trust. It changes our focus from us and what we can do and puts the focus on God and what He can do in us, through us, and for us. Where we feel fearful, He assures us of His power. Where we are discouraged, He gives us courage to know His power. Where we are weak, He gives us the strength for every task. We can tap into the inexhaustible resources which He has available in order for us to combat our fears and to reposition our thinking based on what God does for us. Now that is a resource you do not want to miss out on each and every day. Claim the I AM as a part of your daily prayer life. Know Him and experience His power as you go about your daily living... really living for Him.

Our third verse in this series also comes from later chapters in Isaiah 46:09 and states,

46:09 ***Remember the things I have done in the past. For I alone am God! I am God, and there is none like me. (NLT)***

We greatly value our memories. They help to define us. They are what make us unique as individuals. Some memories really stand out in our minds. Some good...some not so good. In this verse, God is reminding His people (and all of us today) that we should regularly go back through a list of ALL the wonderful things which we have received and been blessed with in the past to see what God has done. It has been a miracle... or several. Too often we dwell on the bad things... our mistakes... failures... hurts... frustrations... relationship issues... you name it. Anything which the devil can drag up, he will... and often. Satan does NOT want us to think about God and what God has done for us. It greatly overshadows and overpowers ALL the sins of the past and it gives us a hope for the future... an eternal future with God. That is why we are to really understand that when we are His... we are a child of God. Wow!! And, He reminds us that He alone is God... not us... not others... not possessions... not power... not fame... not anything else ever! He can state "***there is none like me***" and be totally truthful in that statement... there is nothing and no one who can compare with God. So, this verse reminds us to keep those positive and helpful memories right there at the forefront of our minds. We are to remember whose side we are on AND more importantly, who's on our side!! Then we will know that we serve the one and ONLY true God. Nothing else ever will even come close. Stay close to Him... because the I AM is always with you!

3 Point Checkpoint

- ***3:14*** *Exodus* ***God said to Moses, "I AM WHO I AM. This is what you are to say to the Israelites: 'I AM has sent me to you.'" (NIV)***
- ***41:10*** *Isaiah* ***Don't be afraid, for I am with you. Don't be discouraged, for I am your God. I will strengthen you and help you. I will hold you up with my victorious right hand. (NLT)***
- ***46:09*** *Isaiah* ***Remember the things I have done in the past. For I alone am God! I am God, and there is none like me. (NLT)***

Well done for continuing this far into ***Take Time For God's Word*** *and for getting closer to God by knowing His Word more deeply in your heart and in your mind. That is what these verses represent. Knowing God (I AM). Knowing Him in your heart (the source word for courage means to 'take heart'). Knowing Him in your mind (remembering ALL that He has done for you in the past... and will do for you in the future). You can have a lot of knowledge in this life but without knowing Him, you are really missing out on the best that life has to offer... and it comes with a lifetime (and beyond) guarantee. Don't miss out.*

Know the I AM *(continues)*

Our next verse is the last one that I reference from the Old Testament and comes from Isaiah 48:12 which makes it personal to Jacob,

48:12 ***Listen to me, Jacob, Israel, whom I have called: I am he; I am the first and I am the last. (NIV)***

If you have kids (or have ever been around kids), you will often hear someone saying "listen to me". It is hard to get their attention. It is hard to get them to focus on what you want to tell them. They are in a world unto themselves. Sounds a lot like us! Sounds a lot like Jacob, too. God often reminds us to '***listen***' to Him through His Word. He wants us to stop what we are doing and to give Him some focused time and attention. He deserves it. Yet, we often don't quite get it. That is why he (again) reminds us that we are 'called'. That means we have been specifically set apart. We have a mission. We have a purpose. We have great value to Him. Then, He puts it into a broader perspective***..."I am the first and I am the last".*** Talk about great 'bookends' to life and to all of existence, that about sums it up. Our God was there at the beginning and He will be the one who ties it all together at the very end. So, with those kind of credentials, it makes good sense (actually great sense!) to listen to Him and to hear what He has planned for us in our lives. And not just our lives but what He can do in and through us in the lives of others. We often miss that part. That we are to have influence and impact into the lives of others. We might be the great blessing that they have been praying for. Sometimes, what appears to be a problem or an inconvenience for us may have been an answer to prayer for someone else. Think about it. Consider God's bigger picture to see all the great things He has planned just for you and for your impact in this world. Don't miss out on a single day of it!

Next, we move from the Old Testament into the New Testament and verses which Jesus uses to align Himself with God. These were bold statements which the religious authorities considered blasphemy by claiming that He was God. Yet, that is exactly who Jesus was and is in our lives today. He took on human form to do what no one else could do... So, let's start with 4:26 of John which states,

4:26 ***Then Jesus declared, "I, the one speaking to you—I am he." (NIV)***

When confronted by tough questions or tough challenges, Jesus did not back down. He stated the truth. He stated it boldly. He stated it lovingly. He stated it directly. How about you? Is that how you talk or witness to others? That's why we ALL need to keep on learning more from His Word and about His Word as we grow in faith and maturity. This verse is from Jesus encounter with the woman at the well in Samaria. This woman is surprised that a Jew would talk with her let alone ask her for a drink of water. She states that when the Messiah comes, then He would be able to explain all things to the people. Then Jesus makes this statement in **4:26**. There was no doubt what He meant. And, he makes that claim to the Samaritans... not what they expected. But, that is exactly what they needed. He came to them. He met them where they were. He broke down social and societal barriers. He met with those who others had shunned. He talked plainly with those who needed it most. He became the '***I AM***'... present... right there with them... right there for them... the savior... just like He comes to us today. He comes right where we need Him the most. We need to not only let Him in but we need to let Him reign in our lives. We need to let Him occupy the 'throne' of our heart. Let Him rule the heart and the rest of the mind and body will follow. Let Him in today! Keep Him at the center of your heart and life. You will be glad (forever) that you did!!

The next verse in the series continues in John with a great verse and a greater life-lesson for us all from John 6:35, we read,

6:35 ***Jesus replied, "I am the bread of life. Whoever comes to me will never be hungry again. Whoever believes in me will never be thirsty. (NLT)***

If your house is like ours, one of the questions we get A LOT is, 'when is it time for (...breakfast, lunch, dinner, snack, food, bedtime snack,...you get the picture)'. We are ALWAYS looking out for our next meal, sometimes even before we finish the one we are eating. We are a hungry people. We are hungry for more than just food. We are longing for something that will fill us up emotionally...spiritually...lastingly. We don't like an empty feeling in any part of our being. We work hard and will look anywhere (if we have to) to find something to fill up those areas of void or emptiness. Sometimes we look in the wrong places. Sometimes we choose the wrong things. Sometimes (often times) we mess up. That is why Jesus states it plainly here... ***"never be hungry again"..."will never be thirsty".*** He is the one to satisfy our needs. He will do so now but also for the future. It is hard for us to actually understand that...and to then fully believe that. We often still look elsewhere and find that this is none other than Jesus. We should have known better but we can forget that when we have Jesus, we do have the best, most complete, most satisfying of ALL options. Just like my focus is on 'time'... something we all have equally, Jesus emphasizes "bread" and calls Himself the ***"bread of Life"***. It was something everyone would remember. They would remember it multiple times each day. They associated it with life and sustaining their lives. It was shared with family and friends. It was consumed regularly. It gave strength. It gave comfort. It was a nourishment and it was enjoyable. Sounds like something we should remember as well. So, at dinner tonight or at any meal, when there is bread being served, remember this verse and the '***Bread of Life***' which Jesus is to all who believe. Enjoy each bite!

3 Point Checkpoint

- ***48:12*** *Isaiah* ***Listen to me, Jacob, Israel, whom I have called: I am he; I am the first and I am the last. (NIV)***
- ***4:26*** *John* ***Then Jesus declared, "I, the one speaking to you—I am he." (NIV)***
- ***6:35*** *John* ***Jesus replied, "I am the bread of life. Whoever comes to me will never be hungry again. Whoever believes in me will never be thirsty. (NLT)***

*While the verses cover various texts, there is a sequence that can be easy to remember..."**Listen to me**"..."**Then Jesus declared, "I, the one speaking to you...**"..."**Jesus replied, "I am the bread of life".** We should listen...hear Jesus speaking... then know that He satisfies our every need. Please anchor these to* *times or events in your day and make them part of your life...not just verses that you memorize, words that bring more joy to your life.* ***AND don't forget to pass them on to others...they could use a little encouragement, too!!***

KNOW THE I AM *(CONTINUES)*

The seventh verse in this series is also from John and is found in 8:12 which reads,

> 8:12 ***Again Jesus spoke to them, saying, "I am the light of the world. Whoever follows me will not walk in darkness, but will have the light of life." (ESV)***

The flip of a switch. In our world, that's all it usually takes to have light. It is nearly instantaneous. As we move from room-to-room in our house, we just keep flipping switches. In Jesus day, it was a bit harder to have light available so Jesus claim to 'be light' was most unusual and most welcome. It meant that you could take it with you and that you would have light wherever and whenever you needed it. It meant it would never go out. It meant that you did not need to fear the darkness because you had the "***light of life***" with you when you needed it most. Is that what you need? Are you carrying the "***light***" with you? In most of our homes, we have not only dozens of lights throughout the house, we have several flashlights for when those other lights may fail. When storms come...when emergencies cause outages...when people mess up and cut the power lines...we still need light but we need to find other temporary sources to see us through. When that happens, we light candles (if we can find them ...and the matches) so that we can then find the flashlights. And, then we hope that the batteries in those flashlights are still working...but for how long? It is a those times that we really start to understand what it means to be without light. There are people throughout our world who are daily living in that kind of darkness... both physical and even more importantly, spiritual. That is why this verse and this I AM declaration of Jesus is so critical to us all. We need to know the source and constant, never-changing light which Jesus brings to us. We need to tap into it every day. We need to carry it with us. We need to share it with others. We need to depend on it...AND we do!! Live in the light. Be the light to a world in darkness!!

Our next verse also continues in John with 9:05 which is a terrific way to start your morning by remembering this short verse at **9:05** am. It says,

9:05 ***While I am in the world, I am the light of the world." (NIV)***

In our prior verse, we talked about the personal nature of light... in our homes, in emergencies, etc. For this verse, let's broaden our thinking to not just our world (i.e. friends, family, neighborhood, community, even state)...let's focus on THE world. With BILLIONS of people, it is a big place!! We all compete for resources... food...water...air...energy... etc. But, gladly, there is no competition for God's love which He shared through Christ. There is PLENTY to go around. If you give it away...you get even more... how great is that! We often forget about how things work in God's economy...and His light is a great example of it. It touches every part of this world. It is the same for East or West...North or South... In season or out-of-season...day or night...you-get-the-picture. That is why this short verse is a great one to keep handy (mentally) so that you can be reminded often of just how broad and how extensive God's love is as He wants to be the light to everyone, everywhere, all the time. That's where we come in. Someone still needs to share that light. It needs one-on-one time with others. It may take dozens of people before the light really sinks into a person's life. That's OK. That is why the Holy Spirit is working to prepare hearts to receive the Good News. Our task is to share the light to the world. It is still God's job to use the light to eliminate the darkness of sin from a person's life. Once they see the light and know what He has done for them, they will never want to return to the darkness again. So, continue to focus on His Word (just as you are doing here...great job... keep it up!). Continue to share His love. Continue to be His people to a world that is genuinely 'dying' without Him!

We can easily remember the I AM verses in the New Testament because most all of them come from John's Gospel. The next is from 10:09 John and reads,

10:09 ***I am the gate; whoever enters through me will be saved. They will come in and go out, and find pasture. (NIV)***

This verse should be one that we remember often as we walk through any door or gate in or around our homes. The gate is the entrance which allows us passageway into a place of refuge and safety. It can be open or closed. Jesus provides us with an open gate...a welcomed entry...an invitation to come home. As Jesus is describing this in the context of being the 'good Shepherd', it is a reminder that if you enter, you will be saved. The gate is protected and no one can enter to take you from that safety. The verse further reminds us that we can have passage both in and out and that we can find pasture or places to feed on His Word. That accounts for all the freedoms which we have as followers of Christ. He came to set us free...free from sin...free from guilt...free from old habits and desires. So, when you walk through that doorway every day, you can remember that you can leave the past in the past. You can put out old sins and the painful reminders of a former self and life as if it were putting out the trash. It is forgiven. It is hauled away. You don't need to drag it around in your mind any longer. Enjoy that freedom. Enter through the 'gate' and begin, then continue in the new life.

3 Point Checkpoint

- ***8:12*** *John* ***"Again Jesus spoke to them, saying, "I am the light of the world. Whoever follows me will not walk in darkness, but will have the light of life." " (ESV)***
- ***9:05*** *John* ***"While I am in the world, I am the light of the world." (NIV)***
- ***10:09*** *John* ***"I am the gate; whoever enters through me will be saved. They will come in and go out, and find pasture." (NIV)***

More great verses which remind us that God is with us and that Christ came to set us free from our sins. Two verses cover the ***"light of the world"*** *and one encourages us to enter through the* ***"gate"*** *so that we will be saved. If you are tracking these as time, they fit nicely into a morning routine of* ***8:12... 9:05... 10:09****. Maybe you want to set these up as 'reminders' on your phone so that they create a chime or a vibrate notice to you at these times. Then just glance at your watch or phone to see these verses that you entered as reminders will trigger the memory of them. Take just that quick moment to connect with more of the great I AM verse to give you that encouragement, comfort, and hope as you continue in your day. Just as the phrase "I AM" is always present tense, know that Christ is with you always... here and now... so stay in close contact with Him!!*

Know the I AM *(continues)*

Our 10th verse in this series is one you may have even learned as a child in Sunday School or Vacation Bible School and is found in John 10:11 which says,

10:11 ***"I am the good shepherd: the good shepherd gives his life for the sheep. (KJ2000)***

David knew that the life of a shepherd was not an easy one. It meant being alone for long periods of time away from family and the comforts of a home. It meant being outside in the elements...hot days...cold nights ...rain ...sleet ...you get the picture. It also meant protecting the sheep from any dangers and wild animals which may come your way. So, anyone here interested in a career change... I am sure there are a few openings somewhere. Yet, that is how Christ described himself and His mission on earth... to be our "***good shepherd***" and to make all those sacrifices (and more) to care for us as lost sheep in a dangerous world. We know from other accounts of David's youth that he stood his ground against lions and bears to keep his sheep safe. And, we know that the sheep were really from his father, Jesse, and David was just caring for them... being a good steward over them...on behalf of his father. That is how Jesus describes himself in later chapters as He prays to God to continue to protect and keep those that God has entrusted to Him. So, keep your eyes on the "good shepherd" as He continues to lead, guide, protect, and feed you each day. It will be a great journey and the destination is truly out-of-this-world! Be a blessing to others along the way!

The next verse continues with that same theme of being a 'shepherd' but adds a personal element to it. It is taken from John 10:14 and reads,

10:14 ***"I am the good shepherd; I know my sheep and my sheep know me" (NIV)***

So, by remembering the phrase "***I am the good shepherd***", you will be able to remember two great verses from John. This verse makes it even more personal by adding, "***I know my sheep and my sheep know me***". There is a connection between the shepherd and the sheep. They can tell the difference in His call versus the call (or whistle or yell or whatever techniques may be used) of any other person. When one is missing or wanders off, the shepherd knows exactly which one it is and immediately goes looking for that one and seeks it until it is found, saved, and restored to the rest of the flock. So, do you know His voice? Are you even listening for it? There is a LOT of noise in our world which is all trying to drown out the voice of God which is giving us statements through His Word and through His ministers and ministries. We all have a choice on who or what we listen to each day. We need to continue to stay close to His Word and to regularly meet with and fellowship with other believers who can help us grow in our faith AND so that you can help them grow in theirs. As the body of Christ, we owe it to each other to be there when they need us as the tangible arms and legs and feet of Christ to this world. Know the shepherd. Follow His leading. Do not be deceived. Stay connected with the church and fellowship often.

Next, we look at another great truth as Jesus talks about His role and His mission to us and to our world, as it states in John 11:25,

11:25 ***Jesus said to her, "I am the resurrection and the life. The one who believes in me will live, even though they die; (NIV)***

As you might recognize, this verse comes within the story of Lazarus death and resurrection. Jesus knew that Lazarus was sick. Yet, he stayed where he was continuing His work there for two more days before leaving to go to see Lazarus. It was not that He didn't care, He cared deeply for Lazarus and his sisters, Mary and Martha. But, He knew that no one was beyond His reach. Mary had said, ***'if you had only been here'***...not understanding the true power of Jesus and the true nature of what He could and would do for Lazarus. I am sure that each of you have lost loved ones who have died long before you were ready to let them go. It is painful. It is a hurt that lasts a long time. We miss them. We want to keep them with us. Yet, God has other plans which we do not know or even understand (sometimes). In this case, he called out the name of Lazarus and the dead came back to life. He will one day call our names and we too will rise to a new life in Him. That knowledge and understanding of the resurrection and life through Christ is what separates Christianity from other religions. The fact that God allowed His Son to die for our sins and to raise Him up for our salvation is a gift beyond words. We need to keep our focus at **11:25** am or pm as we put our hope and trust in Him. He will not disappoint. He will not fail. Stay focused on Him!

3 Point Checkpoint

- ***10:11*** *John* ***"I am the good shepherd: the good shepherd gives his life for the sheep. (KJ2000)***
- ***10:14*** *John* ***"I am the good shepherd; I know my sheep and my sheep know me" (NIV)***
- ***11:25*** *John* ***Jesus said to her, "I am the resurrection and the life. The one who believes in me will live, even though they die; (NIV)***

Remember the ***'good shepherd'*** *and the* ***'resurrection'*** *and you will know these three verses. Each of the* ***I AM*** *verses gives us another great blessing to* *add to our thinking and to our memories. We need to remember and repeat these great truths of the Gospel as we go about our daily lives. These will help to form new habits and will be readily there when you need them in times of crisis or just as words of comfort and hope each day. Write them where you can see them often. Make them visible. Make them colorful. Make them part of your daily activities and I know it will make your day go better. Keep His truths close at hand, top of mind, and deep in your heart!*

KNOW THE I AM *(CONTINUES)*

Our last 3 verses in this series continues in John with verse 14:06 which is one of the more troubling verses for many other faiths or religions as it states,

> 14:06 ***Jesus answered, "I am the way and the truth and the life. No one comes to the Father except through me. (NIV)***

The reason why this becomes so troubling to others is that it is very clear that Jesus is ***"the way...the truth...the life"***. It is not 'a way...' There is only ONE WAY! He further emphasizes that ***"No one comes to the Father except through me."*** That is pretty plain. That is very direct. There is not any room for misinterpretation. It is what He said it is. So, many others will argue that Christianity is 'too restrictive' or 'too narrow' or 'not very open' or... the list goes on. What they fail to mention or even grasp is that Christ died for ALL people. It is VERY inclusive! What God requires is that once you believe and accept Christ, that God stays as God...no substitutes, no alternatives, no exceptions. That is why SO MANY struggle. It means you need to make a choice. You need to make a commitment. You need to make the ultimate decision...who will be your God? When we understand that God made for us a way of salvation when we had no other options...He sent Christ to die for us...then giving our lives back to Him seems quite reasonable and a great gift from Him to us. That is why this verse is so important to have in our minds and in our hearts. It is only through knowing Jesus as Savior and Friend that we will ever have salvation and a place in heaven. It is that simple...I did not say easy...but the message is simple. Take it to heart each day. Share it often. Help others to understand what Jesus did and what that means for them. It truly is our only hope!

Our next verse is our last one from the book of John and is from 15:05 which says,

15:05 ***"I am the vine; you are the branches. If you remain in me and I in you, you will bear much fruit; apart from me you can do nothing. (NIV)***

Here Jesus is relating to a people who knew about what it took to grow things in an arid and dry land. It required that the vine or main part of a tree or large bush needed to have a great root system where it could draw in the water and nutrients needed to sustain life. From there, branches could continue to draw all that they needed to be fruitful and to produce at their best levels. In other passages, Jesus talks about being grafted into the vine. In our neighborhood, there is a tree which is made up to two very different species. In the spring, the top half of the tree has white blossoms and the bottom half has a light purple set of blossoms. The leaves are different shapes. They change colors at different times in the fall. Yet, it is still one tree all being feed through one main trunk and root system. That could describe us. We are different. We bloom at different times. We change in different ways. Yet, we are all part of the same tree of life which Jesus provides. As we all know, if a branch is cut off or breaks off, it will quickly die. It needs to be connected to grow and thrive. That is true for us as well. We need to be connected through a church or fellowship group so that we can grow and flourish. We need to share in the needs and blessings with other Christians. If you are not yet connected, please make it a point to find a solid Bible teaching/ preaching church where you can take root and grow. It can make a world of difference once you are fully connected through and with God's people!

Our final verse for this series comes from Revelations 1:08 as we look at end-times and what God has planned for the world. It says,

1:08 ***"I am the Alpha and the Omega," says the Lord God, "who is, and who was, and who is to come, the Almighty." (NIV)***

This verse becomes a great book-end to what started back in Genesis **1:01** and the beginning to now at the end of times. It is also a great conclusion to this book as it reminds us all that God will be there for us at the end... the very end of it all. We can have that great assurance. We can depend on what He has promised. We can know that we will be with Him as we have trusted in Christ. Here we see Him as the I AM and he sets the appropriate timing of ***"who is, who was, and who is to come..."*** where He states the present first, then the past and finally the future. We can only actually live in the present... the past is behind us and a memory which we cannot change. Our decisions in the present are what will determine our future so that must be our emphasis and our focus for ourselves and our families. I know how easy it is to get caught up in planning for our futures...college educations, buying a home, working a career, planning for retirement, etc. It is good to have those goals but the key is to live in the NOW and to make that your best effort and primary focus. That is why **Take Time For God's Word** works to bring God's Word to your hearts and minds NOW because that is where we can make changes. That is where we can have an impact. That is what will guide us into our futures. Knowing Christ as Savior and Friend will make all the difference in the world and in your world. Don't miss out. Make Him your priority today and each day... forever!

3 Point Checkpoint

- ***14:06*** *John* ***Jesus answered, "I am the way and the truth and the life. No one comes to the Father except through me. (NIV)***
- ***15:05*** *John* ***"I am the vine; you are the branches. If you remain in***

me and I in you, you will bear much fruit; apart from me you can do nothing. (NIV)

- ***1:08*** *Revelations* ***<u>"I am the Alpha and the Omega,"</u> says the Lord God, "who is, and who was, and who is to come, the Almighty." (NIV)***

People often say that the last words in a speech or in a book are the ones which the audience remembers the most. I hope that is true here as well. These last verses are a great summary to what this book is all about. It wants to bring you closer to God. It wants you to think of Him and His plans for you often throughout your day. It wants you to experience the great and many blessings which He has planned for you. And it wants you to share His love and your blessings with those around you. So, from these last verses it is... Jesus is the only way to God... stay connected to Him and through His church... God is there with you now and forever!!

So, take a few minutes to thank Him for all His blessings. Make a commitment to think of Him and to remember His Word by reciting a verse (or two) whenever you check the time... any verse will do. <u>Stay close to God and follow His Word!! May God richly bless you now and forever!!</u>

Summary–Know the I AM

Time	Book	Verse
3:14	**Exodus**	***<u>God said to Moses, "I AM WHO I AM</u>. This is what you are to say to the Israelites: 'I AM has sent me to you.'" (NIV)***
41:10	**Isaiah**	***<u>Don't be afraid, for I am with you.</u> Don't be discouraged, for I am your God. I will strengthen you and help you. I will hold you up with my victorious right hand. (NLT)***

Time	Book	Verse
46:09	Isaiah	*Remember the things I have done in the past. For I alone am God! I am God, and there is none like me. (NLT)*
48:12	Isaiah	*Listen to me, Jacob, Israel, whom I have called: I am he; I am the first and I am the last. (NIV)*
4:26	John	*Then Jesus declared, "I, the one speaking to you—I am he." (NIV)*
6:35	John	*Jesus replied, "I am the bread of life. Whoever comes to me will never be hungry again. Whoever believes in me will never be thirsty. (NLT)*
8:12	John	*"Again Jesus spoke to them, saying, "I am the light of the world. Whoever follows me will not walk in darkness, but will have the light of life." " (ESV)*
9:05	John	*"While I am in the world, I am the light of the world." (NIV)*
10:09	John	*"I am the gate; whoever enters through me will be saved. They will come in and go out, and find pasture." (NIV)*
10:11	John	*"I am the good shepherd: the good shepherd gives his life for the sheep. (KJ2000)*
10:14	John	*"I am the good shepherd; I know my sheep and my sheep know me" (NIV)*
11:25	John	*Jesus said to her, "I am the resurrection and the life. The one who believes in me will live, even though they die;" (NIV)*

Time	Book	Verse
14:06	**John**	***Jesus answered, "I am the way and the truth and the life.*** ***No one comes to the Father except through me. (NIV)***
15:05	**John**	***"I am the vine; you are the branches.*** ***If you remain in me and I in you, you will bear much fruit; apart from me you can do nothing. (NIV)***
1:08	**Revelations**	***"I am the Alpha and the Omega,"*** ***says the Lord God, "who is, and who was, and who is to come, the Almighty." (NIV)***

CHAPTER 9

Summary and Reminders

Congratulations!! When you have reached this point, you have covered about 121 verses from 29 books of the Bible. While you may not yet know every one of them, you can know them with a little practice and some tools to help you both remember them AND to help you share them with others. The following table takes all the verses and lists them in sequence by Time. This helps you remember verses from a variety of themes for that hour OR sometimes you will have several verses for the same Hour: Minute (Chapter: Verse). You will be surprised at how often you see that time and remember that verse! That's the habit which you are forming as you **Take Time For God's Word** throughout your day.

This table of verses may be one you want to copy from your eBook and paste to a file so that you can print it. You can then fold it up or pin it up as a visual reference to further your learning process (*See chapter 10 for further ideas*). Use the highlighting tool to mark those that you already know and those which you are focusing on. Use a different highlight color for those that you have shared with others. Sharing is a GREAT way to further reinforce the verse for you AND you may have provided a true blessing to others by introducing or reinforcing that verse with them. The Good News is too great not to be shared with others!

Continue to leverage the added resources found at www.taketimefor-godsword.com and at www.facebook.com/taketimeforgodsword. It is that easy to stay connected to God through His Word... when you check the time, think of a verse!

Verse	Book	Text	Theme	Translation
1:04	**1 Corinthians**	***I give thanks to God always for you because of the grace of God which was given you in Christ Jesus,***	Give Thanks	RSV
1:06	**Philippians**	***"I am confident of this, that the one who began a good work among you will bring it to completion by the day of Jesus Christ."***	Do What's Right	NRSV
1:08	**Revelations**	***"I am the Alpha and the Omega," says the Lord God, "who is, and who was, and who is to come, the Almighty."***	Know the I AM	NIV
1:09	**1 John**	***If we confess our sins, he is faithful and just, and will forgive our sins and cleanse us from all unrighteousness.***	Introduction	RSV
2:04	**Philippians**	***"Let each of you look not to your own interests, but to the interests of others."***	Be a New Creation	NRSV
2:08	**Ephesians**	***For by grace you have been saved through faith, and this not your own doing: it is a gift of God.***	Introduction	NRSV
2:09	**Jonah**	***But I with the voice of thanksgiving will sacrifice to thee; what I have vowed I will pay. Deliverance belongs to the LORD!"***	Give Thanks; Do What's Right	RSV

Verse	Book	Text	Theme	Translation
2:10	**Luke**	***"But the angel said to them, "Do not be afraid. I bring you good news that will cause great joy for all the people."***	Be a New Creation	NIV
2:13	**Luke**	***"And suddenly there was with the angel a multitude of the heavenly host praising God and saying,"***	Give Praise	ESV
2:14	**Luke**	***"Glory to God in the highest, and on earth peace among men with whom he is pleased!"***	Give Praise	ESV
2:20	**Luke**	***"And the shepherds returned, glorifying and praising God for all they had heard and seen, as it had been told them."***	Give Praise	ESV
2:23	**Daniel**	***To thee, O God of my fathers, I give thanks and praise, for thou hast given me wisdom and strength,...***	Give Thanks	RSV
2:26	**Joel**	***"You shall eat in plenty and be satisfied, and praise the name of the LORD your God, who has dealt wondrously with you."***	Give Praise	ESV
3:08	**Acts**	***"And leaping up he stood and walked and entered the temple with them, walking and leaping and praising God."***	Give Praise	ESV
3:10	**Romans**	***'There is no one righteous, not even one;'***	Give Thanks	NIV
3:11	**Luke**	***"In reply he said to them, "Whoever has two coats must share with anyone who has none; and whoever has food must do likewise."***	Do What's Right	NRSV
3:14	**Exodus**	***God said to Moses, "I AM WHO I AM. This is what you are to say to the Israelites: 'I AM has sent me to you.'"***	Know the I AM	NIV

Verse	Book	Text	Theme	Translation
3:16	John	*"For God so loved the world that he gave his one and only Son, that whoever believes in him shall not perish but have eternal life."*	Preface	NIV
3:16	John	*For God so loved the world that he gave his only Son, that whoever believes in him should not perish by have eternal life.*	Introduction	RSV
3:22	Lamentations	*"The steadfast love of the Lord never ceases, his mercies never come to an end; [23] they are new every morning; great is thy faithfulness."*	Be a New Creation	ESV
3:23	Colossians	*"Whatever you do, work at it with all your heart, as working for the Lord, not for human masters,"*	Preface	NIV
4:06	Philippians	*"Do not worry about anything, but in everything by prayer and supplication with thanksgiving let your requests be made known to God."*	Do What's Right	NRSV
4:08	Philippians	*"Finally, brothers, whatever is true, whatever is honorable, whatever is just, whatever is pure, whatever is lovely, whatever is commendable, if there is any excellence, if there is anything worthy of praise, think about these things."*	Give Praise	ESV
4:13	Philippians	*I can do all things through him who strengthens me.*	Introduction	NRSV
4:13	Philippians	*'I can do all things through Christ who strengthens me'.*	Do What's Right	King James 2000 Bible
4:26	John	*Then Jesus declared, "I, the one speaking to you—I am he."*	Know the I AM	NIV

Verse	Book	Text	Theme	Translation
5:03	Matthew	***"Blessed are the poor in spirit,** for theirs is the kingdom of heaven."*	Blessed to be a Blessing	NIV
5:04	Matthew	***"Blessed are those who mourn,** for they will be comforted."*	Blessed to be a Blessing	NIV
5:05	Matthew	***"Blessed are the meek,** for they will inherit the earth."*	Blessed to be a Blessing	NIV
5:06	Matthew	***"Blessed are those who hunger and thirst** for righteousness, for they will be filled."*	Blessed to be a Blessing	NIV
5:07	Matthew	***"Blessed are the merciful,** for they will be shown mercy."*	Blessed to be a Blessing	NIV
5:08	Ephesians	***"For once you were darkness, but now in the Lord you are light.** Live as children of light."*	Do What's Right	NRSV
5:08	Matthew	***"Blessed are the pure in heart,** for they will see God."*	Blessed to be a Blessing	NIV
5:09	Matthew	***"Blessed are the peacemakers,** for they will be called children of God."*	Blessed to be a Blessing	NIV
5:10	Matthew	***"Blessed are those who are persecuted** because of righteousness, for theirs is the kingdom of heaven."*	Blessed to be a Blessing	NIV
5:11	Matthew	***"Blessed are you when people insult you,** persecute you and falsely say all kinds of evil against you because of me."*	Blessed to be a Blessing	NIV
5:12	Matthew	***"Rejoice and be glad,** because great is your reward in heaven, for in the same way they persecuted the prophets who were before you."*	Blessed to be a Blessing	NIV
5:13	Nehemiah	***"...And all the assembly said "Amen"** and praised the LORD. And the people did as they had promised."*	Give Praise	ESV

Verse	Book	Text	Theme	Translation
5:16	Matthew	*"Let your light so shine before men, that they may see your good works and give glory to your Father who is in heaven."*	Give	RSV
5:16	1 Thessalonians	*Rejoice always, (17) pray constantly, (18) give thanks in all circumstances; for this is the will of God in Christ Jesus for you.*	Introduction	RSV
5:17	1 Thessalonians	*Pray continually,*	Be a New Creation	NIV
5:17	2 Corinthians	*"Therefore, if anyone is in Christ, he is a new creation; the old has passed away, behold, the new has come."*	Be a New Creation	ESV
5:42	Matthew	*"Give to him who begs from you, and do not refuse him who would borrow from you."*	Give	RSV
6:09	Galatians	*"And let us not get tired of doing what is right, for after a while we will reap a harvest of blessings if we don't get discouraged and give up."*	Do What's Right	TLB
6:09	Galatians	*"So let us not grow weary in doing what is right, for we will reap at harvest time, if we do not give up."*	Do What's Right	NRSV
6:11	John	*Jesus then took the loaves, and when he had given thanks, he distributed them to those who were seated; so also the fish, as much as they wanted.*	Give Thanks	RSV
6:11	Matthew	*"Give us this day our daily bread;"*	Give	RSV

Verse	Book	Text	Theme	Translation
6:17	Romans	***But thanks be to God,*** ***that you who were once slaves of sin have become obedient from the heart to the standard of teaching to which you were committed,***	Give Thanks	RSV
6:21	Matthew	***For where your treasure is,*** ***there will your heart be also.***	Introduction	RSV
6:29B	Luke	***"...If someone takes your coat,*** ***do not withhold your shirt from them."***	Do What's Right	NIV
6:35	John	***Jesus replied, "I am the bread of life.*** ***Whoever comes to me will never be hungry again. Whoever believes in me will never be thirsty.***	Know the I AM	NLT
7:02	Matthew	***"For in the same way you judge others,*** ***you will be judged, and with the measure you use, it will be measured to you."***	Give	NIV
7:07	Matthew	***"Ask, and it shall be given you;*** ***seek, and you will find; knock, and it will be opened to you."***	Introduction	RSV
7:11	Matthew	***"If you then, who are evil,*** ***know how to give good gifts to your children, how much more will your Father who is in heaven give good things to those who ask him!"***	Give	NIV
7:14	2 Chronicles	***"if my people who are called by my name*** ***humble themselves, pray, seek my face, and turn from their wicked ways, then I will hear from heaven, and will forgive their sin and heal their land."***	Do What's Right	NRSV

Verse	Book	Text	Theme	Translation
7:17	**Psalms**	***I will give to the LORD the thanks** due to his righteousness, and I will sing praise to the name of the LORD, the Most High.*	Give Thanks	
8:12	**John**	***"Again Jesus spoke to them, saying, "I am the light of the world.** Whoever follows me will not walk in darkness, but will have the light of life." "*	Know the I AM	ESV
8:28	**Romans**	***We know that in everything** God works for good with those who love him, who are called according to his purpose.*	Introduction	RSV
8:35	**Romans**	***"Who will separate us from the love of Christ?** Will hardship, or distress, or persecution, or famine, or nakedness, or peril, or sword?"*	Do What's Right	NRSV
9:05	**John**	***"While I am in the world, I am the light of the world."***	Know the I AM	NIV
9:08	**2 Corinthians**	***"And God is able to provide you with every blessing in abundance,** so that by always having enough of everything, you may share abundantly in every good work."*	Do What's Right	NRSV
9:10	**Ecclesiastes**	***"Whatever your hand finds to do,** do it with all your might,"*	Preface	NIV
9:24	**Luke**	***For whoever would save his life will lose it;** and whoever loses his life for my sake, will save it.*	Introduction	RSV
10:08	**Matthew**	***"Heal the sick,** raise the dead, cleanse lepers, cast out demons. You received without paying; give without pay."*	Give	ESV

Verse	Book	Text	Theme	Translation
10:09	**John**	***"I am the gate; whoever enters through me will be saved.** They will come in and go out, and find pasture."*	Know the I AM	NIV
10:11	**John**	***"I am the good shepherd: the good shepherd gives his life** for the sheep.*	Know the I AM	KJ2000
10:11	**John**	***"I am the Good Shepherd,** the good shepherd lays down his life for his sheep"*	Give Praise	NIV
10:11	**John**	***I am the good shepherd.** The good shepherd lays down his life for the sheep.*	Introduction	RSV
10:14	**John**	***"I am the good shepherd; I know my sheep** and my sheep know me"*	Know the I AM	NIV
10:24	**1 Corinthians**	***"Do not seek your own advantage,** but that of the other."*	Do What's Right	NRSV
10:42	**Matthew**	***"And if anyone gives even a cup of cold water** to one of these little ones who is my disciple, truly I tell you, that person will certainly not lose their reward."*	Give	NIV
11:05	**Matthew**	***"the blind receive their sight and the lame walk,** lepers are cleansed and the deaf hear, and the dead are raised up, and the poor have good news preached to them."*	Be a New Creation	ESV
11:06	**Hebrews**	***"And without faith it is impossible to please God,** for whoever would approach him must believe that he exists and that he rewards those who seek him."*	Do What's Right	NRSV

Verse	Book	Text	Theme	Translation
11:25	John	*Jesus said to her, "I am the resurrection and the life. The one who believes in me will live, even though they die;"*	Know the I AM	NIV
11:28	Matthew	*Come to me, all who labor and are heavy laden, and I will give you rest.*	Introduction	RSV
12:10	Romans	*"Love one another with mutual affection; outdo one another in showing honor."*	Do What's Right	NRSV
12:12	Romans	*Be glad for all God is planning for you. Be patient in trouble and prayerful always.*	Introduction	TLB
12:13	Ecclesiastes	*"That's the whole story. Here now is my final conclusion: Fear God and obey his commands, for this is everyone's duty. (14) God will judge us for everything we do, including every secret thing, whether good or bad."*	Be a New Creation	NLT
13:12	Matthew	*"Whoever has will be given more, and they will have an abundance. Whoever does not have, even what they have will be taken from them."*	Give	NIV
13:33	Mark	*"Take heed, watch; for you do not know when the time will come."*	Watch And Pray	RSV
13:34	John	*"A new command I give you: Love one another. As I have loved you, so you must love one another."*	Be a New Creation	NIV
13:44	Matthew	*"The kingdom of heaven is like treasure hidden in a field, which a man found and covered up; then in his joy he goes and sells all that he has and buys that field."*	Watch And Pray	RSV

Verse	Book	Text	Theme	Translation
14:06	**John**	***<u>Jesus answered, "I am the way and the truth and the life.</u> No one comes to the Father except through me.***	Know the I AM	NIV
14:11	**Romans**	***<u>"For it is written, "As I live, says the Lord,</u> every knee shall bow to me, and every tongue shall give praise to God".***	Give Praise	NET
14:12	**Romans**	***"So each of us shall give account of himself to God."***	Give Praise	NET
14:23	**Mark**	***<u>And he took a cup, and when he had given thanks</u> he gave it to them, and they all drank of it.***	Give Thanks	RSV
14:38	**Mark**	***<u>"Watch and pray</u> that you may not enter into temptation; the spirit indeed is willing, but the flesh is weak."***	Watch And Pray	RSV
15:02	**Exodus**	***<u>"The LORD is my strength and my song,</u> and he has become my salvation; this is my God, and I will praise him, my father's God, and I will exalt him."***	Give Praise	ESV
15:05	**John**	***<u>"I am the vine; you are the branches.</u> If you remain in me and I in you, you will bear much fruit; apart from me you can do nothing.***	Know the I AM	NIV
15:10	**Luke**	***<u>"Just so, I tell you, there is joy</u> before the angels of God over one sinner who repents."***	Watch And Pray	RSV
15:30	**Proverbs**	***<u>"The light of the eyes rejoices the heart,</u> and good news refreshes the bones."***	Be a New Creation	ESV
16:16	**Mark**	***<u>"He who believes and is baptized will be saved;</u> but he who does not believe will be condemned."***	Watch And Pray	RSV

Verse	Book	Text	Theme	Translation
16:19	Matthew	*"I will give you the keys of the kingdom of heaven; whatever you bind on earth will be bound in heaven, and whatever you loose on earth will be loosed in heaven."*	Give	NIV
16:24	Matthew	*Then Jesus told his disciples, "If any man would come after me, let him deny himself and take up his cross and follow me."*	Watch And Pray	RSV
16:34	2 Chronicles	*O give thanks to the LORD, for he is good; for his steadfast love endures forever!*	Give Thanks	RSV
17:10	Luke	*"we are not much good as servants, for we have only done what we ought to do".*	Watch And Pray	JB Phillips Translation
17:10	Luke	*"So you also, when you have done all that is commanded you, say, 'We are unworthy servants; we have only done what was our duty.'"*	Watch And Pray	RSV
17:16	Luke	*and he fell on his face at Jesus' feet, giving him thanks. Now he was a Samaritan.*	Give Thanks	RSV
18:20	Matthew	*"For where two or three are gathered in my name, there am I in the midst of them."*	Watch And Pray	RSV
18:41	Luke	*"What do you want me to do for you?" He said, "Lord, let me receive my sight."*	Watch And Pray	RSV
19:05	Revelation	*"And from the throne came a voice crying," Praise our God, all you his servants, you who fear him, small and great."*	Give Praise	ESV
19:40	Luke	*"He answered, "I tell you, if these were silent, the very stones would cry out."*	Watch And Pray	RSV

Verse	Book	Text	Theme	Translation
20:16	Matthew	*"So the last will be first, and the first last."*	Watch And Pray	RSV
20:25	Luke	*"He said to them, "Then render to Caesar the things that are Caesar's, and to God the things that are God's."*	Watch And Pray	RSV
20:35	Acts	*'It is more blessed to give than to receive.'*	Do What's Right	NIV
21:13	Luke	*"This will be a time for you to bear testimony."*	Watch And Pray	RSV
21:22	Matthew	*"And whatever you ask in prayer, you will receive, if you have faith."*	Watch And Pray	RSV
22:27	Luke	*"For which is the greater, one who sits at table, or one who serves? Is it not the one who sits at table? But I am among you as one who serves."*	Watch And Pray	RSV
23:34	Luke	*And Jesus said, "Father, forgive them; for they know not what they do."*	Watch And Pray	RSV
24:35	Matthew	*"Heaven and earth will pass away, but my words will not pass away."*	Watch And Pray	RSV
24:48	Luke	*"You are witnesses of these things."*	Watch And Pray	RSV
26:11A	Matthew	*"The poor you will always have with you..."*	Give	NIV
28:19	Matthew	*"Therefore go and make disciples of all nations, baptizing them in the name of the Father and of the Son and of the Holy Spirit, (20) and teaching them to obey everything I have commanded you. And surely I am with you always, to the very end of the age."*	Give Praise	NIV

Verse	Book	Text	Theme	Translation
31:31	**Jeremiah**	***<u>"Behold, the days are coming,</u> says the LORD, when I will make a new covenant with the house of Israel and the house of Judah,"***	Be a New Creation	ESV
31:32	**Jeremiah**	***<u>"not like the covenant which I made with their fathers</u> when I took them by the hand to bring them out of the land of Egypt, my covenant which they broke, though I was their husband, says the LORD.***	Be a New Creation	ESV
31:33	**Jeremiah**	***"But this is the covenant which I will make with the house of Israel after those days, says the LORD: I will put my law within them, and <u>I will write it upon their hearts; and I will be their God, and they shall be my people.</u>***	Be a New Creation	ESV
31:34	**Jeremiah**	***"And no longer shall each man teach his neighbor and each his brother, saying, 'Know the LORD,' for they shall all know me, from the least of them to the greatest, says the LORD; for I will forgive their iniquity, and <u>I will remember their sin no more."</u>***	Be a New Creation	ESV
41:10	**Isaiah**	***<u>Don't be afraid, for I am with you.</u> Don't be discouraged, for I am your God. I will strengthen you and help you. I will hold you up with my victorious right hand.***	Know the I AM	NLT
46:09	**Isaiah**	***<u>Remember the things I have done in the past</u>. For I alone am God! I am God, and there is none like me.***	Know the I AM	NLT

Verse	Book	Text	Theme	Translation
48:12	**Isaiah**	***Listen to me,* Jacob, Israel, whom I have called: I am he; I am the first and I am the last.**	Know the I AM	NIV
51:10	**Psalm**	***"Create in me a clean heart, O God,* and put a new and right spirit within me."**	Be a New Creation	ESV

CHAPTER 10

25 Tips and Techniques to connect to key Bible verses

We all learn in different ways. Some respond to more visual expressions. Others learn by anchoring facts to numbers, phrases, or objects. Some have a photographic memory (don't we wish). There are many ways which work. With today's technology, there are some tips and tools which make it even easier and more effective regardless of how easy (or hard) it is to remember key verses. These 25 Tips and Techniques (both high-tech and low-tech) may be useful in leveraging technology to help in expanding your memory of favorite Bible Verses. Many techniques are listed for Apple devices or Windows device users but apply to Google, Android, etc. devices and tools as well.

1. **Picture perfect:** Use your smart phone to photograph verses on bookmarks, Facebook posts, Pinterest photos with verses, magazines or printed Bible resources. On your Camera Roll, create an

Album called 'Verses' or 'Bible Verses' or 'TTFGW' (short for Take Time For God's Word, is what I called it) and link these photos of verses to that Album. Edit them to be just that verse… brighten them… etc. Then look through that Album to see how many you know (by heart). Keep reviewing it and adding even more!

2. **Alarming news:** Set an Alarm to the time (i.e. verse) that you want to remember and have it ring at that time. It will cause you to check the time and focus on that verse (until you have it in your mind). Name the Alarm (if it allows) to the Verse (e.g. 12:12 Romans). Set several alarms throughout your day. Once you have those verses now remembered, set other alarms.
3. **Remind me (*again*):** Set Reminders to the time (verse). These can be set to repeat (daily, weekly, etc.). You can type (or cut/ paste) the verse into the text of the reminder so that it displays when the Reminder comes due. (You may even want to set different 'ring tones' for Alarms, Reminders, etc.).
4. **Task Lists:** Set Tasks (same type of setup as Reminders) but this may be for 'new verses' or longer passages. Tasks for each day/ week will help to make this a long-term habit and one which you will use often.
5. **Ready – Action:** Set Action Items (same type of setup as Reminders) but this may be for your favorite verses OR those that you need to work on in daily living (e.g. Deuteronomy **15:10** ***"Give generously to the poor, not grudgingly…"*** (NLT)) Use this option for those that are most important to you or of most immediate value to you.
6. **Make a Note:** Create Notes that list favorite verses or verses from a Theme (e.g. Hope, Forgiveness, Praise, etc.). Just list the reference number (e.g. **5:16** 1 Thessalonians) or add a few words to start the verse (e.g. **"Rejoice Always"….** Yes, that is the whole verse). You can create several lists of Notes with the first line becoming the Title for that Note (e.g. 'Verses' or 'Special Verses') and then add all that you want. (This is a great tool for capturing and reviewing verses).

7. **Meet Me:** Create a Calendar event. Like the Reminders, Tasks, or Actions, you can actually schedule a Calendar meeting, event, etc. on a specific Date/ Time. This will show up in your Calendar and will notify you when it is about to happen. You can set every morning at **7:07** (Matthew) to be, ***"Ask and it will be given to you; seek and you will find; knock and the door will be opened to you."*** (NIV) You can have this repeat every day. What a GREAT way to start the day! Then add others throughout the day at various times. Set the chime/ sound to be something different so that you know what it represents. Maybe even download a ring-tone of a favorite Christian song as a further reminder. I know this will fill up your calendar BUT it's because we are all so busy that we need to have some focused time and attention on meeting up with God throughout the day. It is the MOST important meeting you will have each day, I am sure!
8. **Playing Favorites:** Set your links as Favorites. In your browser, find your best verses (hopefully on **Take Time For God's Word** website) and make them Favorites. Do this for other sites (e.g. Biblegateway.com or Biblehub.com) so that you can get to your saved verses quickly and so that you have a LONG list of favorites to choose from every time you go to Favorites.
9. **The Apps have it:** Download Bible apps. There are many good Bible apps for the mobile devices (i.e. phones, iPods, tablets, laptops, etc.) so that you have the whole Bible with you at all times...maybe even multiple translations. You can create your own list of verses within those apps to come back to and to review from time-to-time. There are other great Bible reading and Bible Study options to use as well. Again, the **Take Time For God's Word** process (and www.taketimeforgodsword.com or on Facebook) are to be only one part of your Spiritual growth. We all need to spend time daily in reading and studying God's Word (and finding new favorite verses which speak to your heart and your needs).
10. **Christian site-ing:** Sign up for other Christian Web sites and their

'verse-of-the-day' or Bible devotions. I know that we all feel that we get too much (junk) email BUT these are really important. Just a quick glance at the verse(s) which they are sharing will be a trigger to you to read that verse OR to **"Take Time..."** for other verses when you see the email(s). At least you will have material worth reading in your email folder... that will be worthwhile all by itself.

11. **Say What?:** Use the Voice Recorder. Most mobile phones (and many newer iPads, laptops, etc.) have Voice Recorders so that you can say the verse you want to remember and then save the file. You can then playback the verse(s) which you recorded so that you are hearing it in your own voice. Once you have it committed to memory, you can erase it and add more (or keep it and build up a whole library of recorded verses which are meaningful and helpful to you.)
12. **Speak Boldly:** Dictate the verse(s) to save them for future reference. The Voice Recorder app on most phones will also translate the spoken words to written words. You can then copy, paste, edit and save them to a file of favorites (or put them in Reminders, Tasks, etc.). That way you are leveraging technology to keep the information in multiple forms (e.g. sound, print, pictures, etc.). It truly does help in the memorization process when we can leverage other senses as the imprinting of these verses will be stronger AND the triggers to remember them will be more frequent and active.
13. **Color my world:** Make them colorful! Once you have verses as text (through any input, copy/ paste, etc.), you can then use various colors of letters so that they stand out in your mind....(just like in the 'old' King James Bibles, the words of Jesus were always in red... they stood out as being more important). Maybe **purple** is a favorite color so that several of your most favorite verses are in purple. When you see the color purple (which you probably see quite often), you will likely think of one or more of these verses. Maybe a friend or relative (maybe a parent who has passed away) loved **green** so that you create some verses in green. Seeing that

color will trigger a memory of the verse(s) that they loved and will also trigger thoughts of them and their influence on your life.

14. **Be Bold and Beautiful**: With the MANY choices of fonts, styles, and sizes, you can make your choice of verses to be 40 pt. type to really make it stand out. It can be in various type fonts/ styles based on how you think of that verse. Then whenever you see that style (e.g. *Calligraphy*) it will also help to trigger your thinking back to that verse and what it says to you in that moment. We all relate to a variety of things that make it personal to us. Be creative. Be expressive. Be to the glory of God!
15. **My handsome 'prints':** (Bad pun, sorry, but a practical idea). Make them visible and print them. Ok, so this may seem 'low-tech' to some of you BUT I have a bulletin board (you know, the cork kind) at home with LOTS of printed verses tacked up there. Whenever I look up from my computer, there it is. And, often throughout the day, different verses (and colors and font sizes) get my attention and I love remembering and repeating those verses. While I know society is working to become paperless (and we have be trying for about 30 years now... not there yet, I can assure you), it is OK to print your favorites and to use those as opportunities to bring to mind all the blessings and promises which God has for you in Christ.
16. **Magnetic personality?:** Make them magnetic. Ok, I know that your ink-on-paper is not magnetic BUT I am sure that you already have a refrigerator full of magnets from vacations, ads, clips, etc. So, take your favorites which you printed (or get samples from www.taketimeforgodsword.com/samples) and hang them up as a visual reminder to you throughout the day. When you think you know it, move it to another part of the refrigerator (e.g. side, door, even the back) just to test your memory to see if you truly have it. These verses may be the best material which you have hanging up there AND it is a witness and testimony to those who may come into your house. They may comment about them and you may get to share your faith with others AND you will have many new verses

to use and share with them. You may even want to take down the printed verse and give it to them for their refrigerator. It is OK to pass it on... that is what we are called to do.

17. **Permanent Markers:** Make them permanent. You may have a 'life verse' (mine are Romans 12:12 and 2 Cor 6:9-10, in case you didn't know that about me) and you may want it framed and placed on a wall or mirror or someplace prominent in your home. It is not that you don't know the verse, it is just that you want others to know that that verse is just so precious and special to you. (And it is OK to have multiple 'life verses'... it is not greedy, just part of that abundant life that we are all called to lead).
18. **Carrying it out:** Make them portable. It is great to carry God's Word with you at all times. Bible apps on the phone are great. The phone doesn't weigh any more if you use up all 16G, 32G, 64G, etc. of storage, so load it up. Also, there are several different formats for printing verses (see www.taketimeforgodsword.com/samples). There are folding cards (which fold to the size of a credit card). There are 'bill size' formats (which are the size of a US dollar bill (almost)). And if you print them on colorful paper (e.g. neon green), you can't miss them whenever you take out a credit card or pull out cash for buying something. It is just another way to bring to mind a verse or verses from God's Word to re-mind you of who you are and whose you are. Try it. It works great!!
19. **Let me Repeat:** Make it repeat often. To take idea number 1 (i.e. Photograph verses) one step further, once you have built up a library of photos of the verses (from cards, bookmarks that come in the mail, calendar pages which have verses and great photos on them, Facebook posts, Pinterest, etc.), you can save those to a jump drive, an SD card, or other format memory cards. Then, you can insert those into the electronic 'photo frame' devices so that these repeat throughout the day. You can set it on 30 second or 1 minute intervals so that throughout the day, while in the kitchen (as an example), you are seeing these verses and seeing them change over

and over again. You will soon just glance at a verse and you will remember it and say it to yourself. What a great encouragement to have throughout the day.

20. **Wall-to-Wall:** Make it your wallpaper. Ok, not the literal wall 'wallpaper' (but that would be very creative), the screen saver or wallpaper on your computer or mobile device. It can be just one verse or a picture with a verse on it OR you can make a collage of many favorite verses to be saved as one image (e.g. using MS PowerPoint or other tools to put several images into one composite). That way, when you look at it, you are seeing lots of favorite verses. As you see them, some will stand out as those may be the ones which are speaking to your situation at that time.
21. **Remember TTFGW:** Check out www.taketimeforgodsword.com often. The site has the digital time displayed which then causes the Verse at the bottom of the Home page to change with the time(s) of day. No, there is not a verse for every minute of every hour in a day (at least not yet). But, it does change frequently and it may be a good way for you to find some new verses by checking back often throughout the day and throughout each week. If you have favorites which are not yet listed, please put them in the 'contact us' email and we will work to get them added. We are always looking to expand our reference base for our members. We are still learning with you and we love it!
22. **Keys to learning:** Put the verse number or reference on your keychain (just a label or sticker will do). Some of you may already have a verse or cross or other symbol attached to your keys. Use that as a 'trigger' to a favorite verse or to cause you to check the time to trigger a verse memory. This works for other items as well (e.g. hat, coats, gloves, shoes, etc.) Link those verses to items of clothing and repeat it each morning / evening when changing. Maybe it is associated with objects in your house or work (e.g. door, stairs, lamp, etc.) when you see them, it will trigger a verse and soon you will know it... then add another.

23. **Let it show:** Put it on your license plate frame OR as a Personal License Plate number (e.g. **JOHN 316** would be great!!). That way you will be reminded when you drive and so will the car behind you in traffic. If it is bumper-to-bumper, they will learn it in just one commute and you may be witnessing to dozens of different people every day. Maybe it is a bumper sticker or a 'fish' emblem or other Christian symbol that helps trigger a verse for you... and maybe it will for other believers as well. **5:16** Matthew, **"Let your light so shine before others..."** (NIV)
24. **Put on the whole armor:** Maybe it is **'putting on the whole armor'** from Ephesians 6:13-17 and that is a shirt or hat with your verse on it as well. There are various Christian stores (and web sites) which may have some of these now (and maybe the TTFGW.org site will someday, too). It is a way to give a 'silent testimony' which speaks volumes to others about what you believe in. Sure, you may get a comment or two from others who are non-believers BUT at least you know they were presented with the word of God today! That's a start. Then keep praying for them. Truly they need all the help we can give for them to make a change in their lives. **6:17** Ephesians **"Take the helmet of salvation and the sword of the Spirit, which is the word of God." (NIV)** *(Underline is for my emphasis).*
25. **Pin it on:** No, not Pinterest (although that is not a bad idea either... we will work on that). I was thinking about pins for your lapel or dress or just to have on a jacket. Many years ago at a Bible Camp where I was Program Director (i.e. Riverside Lutheran Bible Camp, Story City, IA), we had a button machine were we could design buttons and then press them out. One just said 'RA' with the small print of 1 Thess 5:16 ("Rejoice Always."). Others just had verse numbers (e.g. Romans 8:28) on them. Again, you can be creative on what and how you may want to use this option to help you (and others) to add more meaningful verses to your vocabulary.

So, that's 25 ways that you can use with some high-tech and low-tech options to help you in focusing on some key verses and putting them where you are bound to see them or hear them throughout your day. The key is to **Take Time For God's Word** many times during your daily activities. Just because we get busy and forget about Him, He is always thinking about us.

If you have other ideas and if you want to share them, please let us know at editor@taketimeforgodsword.com and we will try to add to this list through blogs or links in the future.

Acknowledgements

While there are many people who have helped encourage and shape this work, I am deeply indebted to Rev Charles S. Mueller, Sr. for his continual encouragement and support within the Bible Study processes at Trinity Lutheran Church in Roselle, Illinois. I am truly forever in your debt and I pray that this outreach ministry will have blessings multiplied as it finds a place in people's hearts and minds and lives.

Thanks also to the great friends and supporters in the Trinity Bible Study group for their patience in providing needed feedback, ideas, and encouragement to me through the years in developing and sharing these verses and this process with them. They truly are forever friends!

I also owe great thanks and appreciation to my wife, Jan, who allowed me the hours upon hours of research, study, and writing while she kept the rest of our lives operating well. All my love, always!

Great thanks to Steve Harrison at Bradley Communications and to all the coaches who shared their wisdom and insights in writing and promoting this book. Excellent support and guidance.

AND, special thanks to you, my new friends and readers. I look forward to your ideas, feedback, and your own personal experiences which we can share with others in the community of believers. May God richly bless you on your journey with Him every day.

Let me know your comments through www.taketimeforgodsword.com or on Facebook at www.facebook.com/taketimeforgodsword. Check both locations for frequent news, blogs and posts which provide other great memory verses and ideas as you continue the life-long process of knowing God and his plans for you. Share it with your family and friends. It could be a life-changing event for them.

References

The following are some of the key resources and references which were used throughout this book. I have included links where possible so that you can find out more information or so that you can download more materials from those sites.

Bible Translations

The following were the primary Bible Translations used and referenced in this book.

- **English Standard Version (ESV).**

  The Holy Bible, English Standard Version® (ESV®)Copyright © 2001 by Crossway,a publishing ministry of Good News Publishers.All rights reserved.ESV® Text Edition: 2016
  https://www.crossway.org/support/esv-bible-permissions/
  "Scripture quotations are from the ESV® Bible (The Holy Bible, English Standard Version®), copyright © 2001 by Crossway, a publishing ministry of Good News Publishers. Used by permission. All rights reserved."

- **J.B. Phillips Translation of the New Testament.**

  The New Testament in Modern English by J.B Phillips copyright © 1960, 1972 J. B. Phillips. Administered by The Archbishops' Council of the Church of England. Used by Permission.

- **King James 2000.**

  King James 2000. A minimal update of the King James Version (c)2011. Thelma J. Couric. www.kingjames2000.com All rights reserved. Scripture quoted by permission.

- **NET Bible.**

  "Scripture quoted by permission. All scripture quotations, unless otherwise indicated, aretaken from the NET Bible® copyright ©1996-2016 by Biblical Studies Press, L.L.C.All rights reserved."

  http://netbible.com/net-bible-copyright

- **The New King James Version**

  Scripture taken from the New King James Version®. Copyright © 1982 by Thomas Nelson. Used by permission. All rights reserved.

- **New International Version (NIV).**

  THE HOLY BIBLE, NEW INTERNATIONAL VERSION®, NIV® Copyright © 1973, 1978, 1984, 2011 by Biblica, Inc.® Used by permission. All rights reserved worldwide.

  These Scriptures are copyrighted by the Biblica, Inc.® and have been made available on the Internet for your personal use only. Any other use including, but not limited to, copying or reposting on the Internet is prohibited. These Scriptures may not be altered or modified in any form and must remain in their original context. These Scriptures may not be sold or otherwise offered for sale.

  These Scriptures are not shareware and may not be duplicated.

  When quotations from the NIV text are used in non-salable media such as church bulletins, orders of service, posters, transparencies or similar media, a complete copyright notice is not required, but the initial NIV must appear at the end of each quotation.

  Any commentary or other Biblical reference work produced for commercial sale that uses the New International Version must obtain written permission for the use of the NIV text.

  Permission requests for commercial use within the U.S. and Canada that exceed the above guidelines must be directed to, and approved in writing by, HarperCollins Christian Publishing, Attention: Permissions Department, P.O. Box 141000, Nashville, TN 37214.

https://www.biblegateway.com/versions/New-International-Version-NIV-Bible/#copy

- **New Living Translation (NLT)**

  https://www.biblegateway.com/versions/New-Living-Translation-NLT-Bible/#copy

- **New Revised Standard Version (NRSV) / Revised Standard Version (RSV).**

  For additional information on RSV and NRSV copyright and licensing policies, please see the information posted at: http://www.nrsv.net/contact/licensing-permissions/

- **The Living Bible (TLB).**

Publishers, Inc., Carol Stream, Illinois 60188. All rights reserved. *https://www.tyndale.com/permissions*

Chapter 1 – Be Blessed to Be a Blessing

1. *Merriam-Webster*. Merriam-Webster, n.d. Web. 18 Oct. 2016. www.merriam-webster.com

Chapter 2 – Give – for giving is Living

1. Warren, Richard. *The Purpose-driven Life: What on Earth Am I Here For?* Grand Rapids, MI: Zondervan, 2002. Print.
2. Wilkinson, Bruce, and Brian Smith. *Beyond Jabez*. Sisters, Or.: Multnomah, 2005. Print.
3. Wilkinson, Bruce. *The Prayer of Jabez: Breaking through to the Blessed Life*. Sisters, Or.: Multnomah, 2000. Print.

Chapter 4 – Give Praise

Blonde Christian Song. (Songwriter unknown to me).

Chapter 6 – Do What's Right

1. Trinity Lutheran Church. 405 Rush Street, Roselle, IL 60172-2294. Main phone: 630-894-3263. Main fax: 630-894-1430. www.trinityroselle.com
2. McFerrin, Bobby. *Don't Worry, Be Happy*. Cema Special Markets, 1993. CD.
3. *Mad Magazine (http://www.madmagazine.com/) or (http://www.dcentertainment.com/about-dc-entertainment)*
4. *Riverside Lutheran Bible Camp. 3001 Riverside Road, Story City, IA 50248. Main phone: 800-372-7748. Main fax: 515-733-4096. www.RiversideLBC.org.*

5. Card, Michael. *Heal Our Land*. Sparrow Corp., 1993. CD.
6. *Voltaire quote. http://spirous5.blogspot.com/*
7. Ziglar, Zig. *Quotes from Zig Ziglar: Inspire to Be Great!* N.p.: n.p., n.d. Print.
8. *Pat Robertson. http://www.patrobertson.com/*

Chapter 7 – Watch And Pray

1. "Explore Our Online Programs." *Waldorf University*. N.p., n.d. Web. 18 Oct. 2016. *www.waldorf.edu*
2. *Lutheran Youth Encounter (LYE). http://www.youthencounter.org/blog/6153/youth-encounter-closing-its-doors/*
3. *Fried Green Tomatoes*. Dir. Jon Avnet. Prod. Jon Avnet. By Fannie Flagg. Perf. Kathy Bates, Jessica Tandy, and Mary Stuart Masterson. Universal Pictures, 1991. Film.

Chapter 8 – Know the "I AM"

1. Houghton, Israel, Benton Brown, and Jimmy Needham. *I Am Free Worship Collection*. Naxos Digital Services/Inpop, 2009. CD.

Resources

There are a number of samples which can be downloaded or just printed from the website at:

www.taketimeforgodsword.com/samples

Please check back frequently for other new or added updates to that site.

Also, check out the daily verse postings on

www.facebook.com/taketimeforgodsword

Please sign up for a series of free emails and new materials at:

www.davidapedersen.com

Share your thoughts with others!!

Please take a few minutes to write a Review on Amazon about what you found most helpful in the book.

You will help me to become a better author and you will help to encourage potential readers to invest their time to reading this book.

THANK YOU! You are a great blessing to me and to others around you.

David A. Pedersen

About the Author

David A. Pedersen is a Christian author and speaker who is passionate about helping mature Christians grow deeper in their faith by knowing God's Word more personally. He has always been interested in writing and earned degrees (BS/ MS) in Journalism / Advertising from Iowa State University and Journalism/ Public Relations from Northern Illinois University. Another great interest became his 40+ year career in technology and computers as he worked for some of the largest health insurance and software and consulting firms during his executive leadership years in that field. He has accumulated (endured) more than 3.2 million air miles and more than 2500 nights of hotel stays as he spent time at his clients during his long career as a consultant.

David has had a variety of roles in youth ministry, Bible Camp ministries, Sunday School teaching, Bible Study leader, and more. It was through these wide-ranging activities working with a variety of age groups that he developed a love of key Bible verses across several translations. He is continually finding 'new' verses that now have greater meaning at this stage of his life. It is those 'aha' moments which compel him to continue to write and to share these findings with his publishing and social networks.

When he has available time, David and his wife, Jan, enjoy travels and cruises to various parts of the world. Some of those settings have added to his inspiration and have given him time to reflect on new themes and verses. He splits his time between Florida and Chicago. When not traveling, he enjoys spending time with his adult children and two granddaughters in the Chicago area. As a native of Iowa, he still visits family and friends in his home state and enjoys nurturing his Norwegian heritage with favorite recipes (but NOT lutefisk).

His simple process and compelling stories help you to relate to Bible verses in ways that become unforgettable. Find out about the latest activities at **www.davidapedersen.com** or track daily postings on Facebook at **www.facebook.com/taketimeforgodsword**. David can also be reached through Prescott and Radcliffe Press, P.O. Box 191, Bloomingdale, IL 60108.

Stay blessed and pass it on!

Made in the USA
Columbia, SC
02 February 2021